THE THEOLOGY OF ILLNESS

The
THEOLOGY
of
ILLNESS

JEAN-CLAUDE LARCHET

translated by John & Michael Breck

ST VLADIMIR'S SEMINARY PRESS
CRESTWOOD, NEW YORK

Library of Congress Cataloging-in-Publication Data

Larchet, Jean-Claude, 1949–
    [Théologie de la maladie. English]
    Theology of illness / Jean-Claude Larchet ; translated by John & Michael Breck
        p.   cm.
    Includes bibliographical references.
    ISBN 0-88141-239-2
        1. Diseases—Religious aspects—Orthodox Eastern Church.   2. Spiritual healing.
    I. Title.

    BX323.L3713 2002
    261.8'321—dc21

                                                                    2001059157

The Theology of Illness

ST VLADIMIR'S SEMINARY PRESS
575 Scarsdale Rd, Crestwood, NY 10707
1-800-204-2665

Originally published in French
by Les Éditions du Cerf, 1991,
under the title *La Théologie de la Maladie.*

ISBN 0-88141-239-2

PRINTED IN THE UNITED STATES OF AMERICA

Contents

Foreword   7

Introduction   9

1. *The Origins of Illness*
   The Original "Perfection"   17
   The Initial Cause of Illness: Original Sin   26
   Are People Responsible for the Illnesses
        That Afflict Them?   33
   The Healing of Human Nature by the Incarnate Word   40
   Why Does Illness Persist?   41
   Illnesses of the Body and Illnesses of the Soul   50
   The Precariousness of Health   53

2. *The Spiritual Meaning of Illness*
   The Ambivalence of Health and Illness   55
   The Positive Meaning of Sickness and Suffering   57
   A Manifestation of Providence   60
   An Opportunity for Spiritual Progress   64
   God's Help and Man's Contribution   69
   The Importance of Patience   71
   The Essential Role of Prayer   72
   The Way of Holiness   76

3. *Christian Paths toward Healing*

Seek Healing to Glorify God   79

Christ the Physician   81

The Saints Heal in the Name of Christ   84

Spiritual Paths Toward Healing   85

The Role of Secular Medicine   102

Maximalist Positions   109

A Spiritual Understanding of Secular Means of Healing   114

Healing Comes from God   116

The Limitations of Medical Science   119

Have a Care also for the Healing of the Soul   121

The Healing of the Body Symbolizes and Foretells
the Healing of Our Whole Being   124

Illnesses of the Soul Are More Serious than
Those of the Body   125

The Relative Nature of Physical Health   126

The Promise of Future Incorruptibility and Immortality   126

Christ Came also to Save the Body   127

Foreword

Publication in the middle of the last century of C.S. Lewis' classic study, *The Problem of Pain*, gave rise to a great deal of profound reflection in Christian circles on the entire matter of suffering, particularly on what is perceived as "innocent" suffering. Since that time a large number of works have appeared which focus that reflection in diverse areas. Very little has been produced, however, on the origins and meaning of human illness as such: the sickness of both body and soul.

A major exception to that trend is the work of the French Orthodox teacher and scholar, Jean-Claude Larchet. From his monumental doctoral dissertation, *Thérapeutique des maladies spirituelles* (second edition 1993, 946 pages!), until the present, Larchet has focused especially on questions of illness, together with spiritual therapies developed within the Church that seek their cure. His theological interests, however, are by no means limited to this particular issue. He has produced as well serious and valuable studies on subjects as varied as St. Maximus the Confessor and the contemporary Orthodox-Catholic debate over the *filioque* clause in the Western version of the Nicene-Constantinopolitan Creed.

The present work, *The Theology of Illness*, originally appeared in 1991. Like all of the author's published writings, it is permeated with the wisdom of the Holy Fathers of the Greek patristic tradition, while it draws heavily from Scripture and Orthodox liturgical sources. Nevertheless, it is not intended to be a scholarly study. It aims, rather, at delving at a layperson's level into one of the most difficult and burdensome problems in human experience: the origins and ultimate meaning of physical illness. Each of us is in the grip of a "sickness unto death." This book provides a fresh look at the origins and significance of that sickness. Then it indicates the way toward genuine, spiritual health, which is attained finally in the Kingdom of Heaven by the grace and mercy of a suffering God.

The author begins with consideration of the relation between

sickness and sin, providing a traditional yet refreshingly contemporary view of human nature and the human person. The questions he
considers are fundamental: the origins of sin in a fallen world, its
impact on physical health, and the healing of human nature by the
incarnate Son of God. In the second chapter, he discusses the positive value of illness: how it can engender spiritual growth, patience
and prayer. Finally, he takes up the matter of healing as a means of
glorifying God, stressing again the crucial role of prayer and sacramental grace in promoting genuine health.

Throughout this work, Dr Larchet carefully situates spiritual
growth and physical healing within the context of the Church's ministry and the Church's life. His perspective is profoundly ecclesial: the
pathway to Christian wholeness and health involves the ill person not
as an isolated individual but as a member of the universal Body of
Christ.

This pathway to Christian healing has been fully charted by
Orthodox Christianity since early patristic times, with the creation of
hospitals and hospices, together with the ministry of those we venerate as "holy unmercenary saints." As the author shows, there exists an
essential continuity between the theological reflections and practical
responses of the Church Fathers to the phenomenon of illness and
the various approaches to medicine and therapy developed in our own
day. Therefore he can underscore the benefits of modern medicine
and the appropriateness of its use, while affirming that all true healing is a gift, bestowed by the God of love and compassion.

We are grateful that this book, already translated into many lan-
guages, has now appeared in English. It is a work that offers us fresh
insight into the mystery of evil, sin and illness, and their place within
our struggle toward holiness. It provides us with a deep understanding of the biblical and patristic perspective on sickness and redemptive suffering, in our own lives and in the lives of all those for whom
we pray. Above all, it gives us renewed hope, by locating the "problem
of pain" in a profoundly theological framework, in which ultimate res-
olution of the mystery of illness and suffering is provided by the healing touch of Christ Himself, the Physician of our souls and bodies.

—*Fr John Breck*

Introduction

There is no one who, in the course of a lifetime, has not had to face some form of illness. Illness is inevitably linked to the human condition. No organism is perfectly healthy. And health itself is never more than a temporary balance between the forces of life and other forces that oppose them, since the supremacy of the former is tentative and fragile.

Life, it has been said, "is by its very nature a temporary staying of death. Every one of our cells is preserved at the cost of an ongoing struggle with forces that tend to destroy it. From our youth, our tissues include large areas subject to deterioration and general wear and tear. From our birth, human cells contain the seeds of their own destruction . . . Sickness marks the whole of our fleshly life. Even under the guise of health, biological phenomena constantly pass beyond the limits of what is 'normal.' Medical professionals constantly observe the fact that physical processes leading to morbidity are combined with the most basic life-functions."[1] Even when we believe we are in good health, illness is potentially there within us, and it merely requires the weakening of one of our systems of *defense* for it to appear in one form or another. And at times, before we are even aware of it, it has done considerable damage.

Every form of illness causes suffering. Most cause us to suffer both physically and psychologically. All of them create spiritual suffering, since they reveal, sometimes with a certain cruelty, the fragile nature of our condition. They remind us that health and biological life are not "goods" that we can hold on to forever, but that in this world our body is destined to diminish, to deteriorate, and finally to die.

From this perspective, illness poses a number of inescapable

---

[1]Marcel Sendrail, *Histoire culturelle de la maladie* (Toulouse, 1980), p. 2.

questions: Why? Why me? Why now? For how long? What is to become of me?

Every illness represents a questioning of ourselves that is intense and preoccupying by virtue of the fact that it is neither abstract nor benign, but represents an often tormenting attack on our very being. This questioning is often critical. For illness always calls into question the basis, the framework and the shape of our lives, including the life-patterns we have acquired, the free use of our bodily and psychological faculties, our system of values, our relations with other people, even life itself. This is because in times of illness the inevitability of death becomes a stark reality.

Far from being an event that touches only our body, and that for a limited time, illness often forces us to assume a spiritual struggle that involves our whole being and destiny. One way or another, we must overcome this trial by assuming the illness and the various forms of suffering that accompany it, by finding solutions to it, solutions that are theoretical but especially practical. Each of us, in the course of our life, has not only to take into consideration sickness and suffering in a theoretical way, but when they occur, we need to find a means for continuing to live, while discovering in them or in spite of them our personal fulfillment.

That, of course, is never easy. Illness normally plunges us into unfamiliar territory, where the conditions of our life are significantly modified and where our relationships with those around us are disturbed and often weakened by imposed isolation. In such cases, we are obliged to deal not only with physical pain, but with anxiety and discouragement, even anguish and despair. This simply increases our sense of solitude, since we feel so very much alone in our efforts to confront the situation.

And there is no question that people today have far fewer resources than their ancestors did to deal with the entire problem.

Without question, modern medicine has attained a remarkably high degree of scientific knowledge, technical ability and social organization. It has attained an extraordinary degree of effectiveness in the realms of prevention, diagnosis and therapy. A great many illnesses that in ages past decimated populations have virtually disappeared in recent years. Today we can count on rapid healing from afflictions that our ancestors had to endure long-term, or that were wholly incurable. Today we can be relieved of forms of suffering that used to be inevitable. Yet we have to admit that this progress has its limits, and even its failures, due less to medicine itself than to various values—or ideologies—that in certain cases underlie its application and development.

The development of medicine in a purely naturalist perspective served to objectify illness, making of it a reality considered in itself and for itself. Illness came to be construed as uniquely physiological and somehow independent of the afflicted person. Rather than treat the person, many physicians today treat illnesses or organs. This fact—complicated by diagnostic methods that are increasingly quantitative and abstract, together with therapeutic methods that are more and more technical—has had as its primary consequence the effect of considerably depersonalizing medical practice. This factor, of course, only increases the distress and isolation of the ill person. A second consequence has been to divest patients of their illness and their suffering, thereby limiting their means for dealing with them. By regarding sickness and suffering as autonomous realities of a purely physiological character—and consequently as susceptible to treatment that is purely technical, applied to the body alone—modern medicine does practically nothing to help patients assume them. Rather, it encourages patients to consider that both their state and their fate lie entirely in the hands of the physicians, that the only solution to their troubles is purely medical, and that the only way they can endure their suffering is to look passively to medicine for any hope of relief and healing.

The dominant values of modern Western civilization, as a matter of fact, encourage just such an attitude. The overvaluation of biological life, considered as the only form of life possible for man; psychological health considered as the enjoyment of a state of well-being conceived in almost exclusively material terms, of which the body appears as the essential organ; the fear of all that can endanger, reduce or eliminate that enjoyment; the refusal of all forms of suffering and the suppression of pain as the highest value of civilization and the consummation of social development;[2] the fear of biological death considered as the absolute end of human existence: all of this leads a great many of our contemporaries to expect that salvation comes from medicine and encourages them to make of the physician a new priest of modern times,[3] a king who holds over them the power of life or death, and a prophet of their ultimate destiny. All this explains as well the absurdity of certain current medical, biological and genetic practices that do not, as is sometimes thought, result from a natural development of science and technology. They are instead an expression of the spirit of the times, which serve to satisfy its demands and speak to its anxieties.

The hope, born at the close of the 18th century, that sickness and suffering would totally disappear in a trouble-free society restored to its original state of health[4]—a hope associated with belief in the continual progress of science and technology—is more alive than ever. Present developments in the field of genetics has allowed us to add to that hope a certain faith in the possibility that by appropriate manipulations human nature can be biologically purified of its imperfections, and that perhaps even death itself can be finally overcome.

Without doubt, these attitudes bear witness to positive aspirations that are deeply rooted in human nature: that man might escape death, which he rightly considers as foreign to his true nature, that he might escape the limits of his present condition, and that he might attain a form of life free of imperfections, where he can grow, free of limitations. But isn't it an illusion to expect from medical and biological sciences and techniques a response that can really satisfy such aspirations?

We should note in the first instance that if many illnesses have disappeared thanks to medical progress, others have appeared to take their place.[5] The average life-span has been significantly increased in

---

[2]This point has been stressed, with a certain polemical excess, by I. Illich, *Némésis médical* (Paris, 1975), ch. 6.

[3]See M. Foucault, *Naissance de la clinique. Une archéologie du savoir médical* (Paris 1972), I. Illich, *op.cit.*

[4]Cf. M. Foucault, *op. cit.*

[5]Cf. M. Sendrail, *op. cit.*, ch. 18.

developed countries, thanks to medical progress as well as to a general improvement in the material conditions of living. But that increase has remained static in recent years, revealing limits that are more and more difficult to surpass. This is apart from the fact that statistically measured "life expectancy" means nothing for the individual, who is in no way bound by statistical "laws." And it leaves aside as well the fact that a significant cause of pathologies and mortality rates today is *accidents*, which by their very nature are unforeseeable, and which by the sheer number of their victims recall the effects of past epidemics.

As for suffering, although certain treatments today can eliminate or at least effectively reduce it, they are unable to do so completely when it is intense, without diminishing, modifying or suppressing the patient's consciousness, thereby further limiting his or her personal freedom. This in itself makes clear the fragile basis on which the hopes of modern man are constructed. To the enduring myth of perfect health there replies the reality, experienced daily by millions of people, of sickness, suffering and death that often intrude into their lives "like a thief in the night."

In addition, it is important to recognize the fact that the new medical, biological and genetic technologies pose more problems than they resolve. The "brave new world" they might be able to create, if no limit is imposed upon them, looks more like hell than like the paradise quested after by those who trust blindly in them. It seems, in fact, that these technologies are developing in such a way as to lead to a growing depersonalization. This is because they transform human illnesses and suffering into independent events and purely technical problems; because they at times make of the human person an object of experimentation, and thus aim less at relieving the person than at scientific progress and at technology considered as an end in itself; and because they minimize the importance of personal relationships and fundamental human values which are vital to the existence of every person, from conception to death.

To this we need to add the fact that most medical practices today have as their common denominator the consideration of the human person as a purely biological organism or, in the best of cases, as a

body as person

simple psycho-somatic entity. For this reason, despite their effectiveness on a certain level, they can only have, on another more fundamental level, effects that are profoundly negative, since they
implicitly disregard the spiritual dimension that essentially characterizes every human being. Although the human body, in its biological reality, is subject to laws that govern the functioning of every
living organism, the body can not be treated just like any other living
organism, since it is the body of a human person from which it cannot be dissociated without losing its very nature. In its present conditions of existence, the body is inseparable not only from a complex
psychological element that in itself elevates man well above animals;
it is also inseparable from a spiritual dimension that is more basic than
its biological aspect. The body does not only express the person; to a
certain extent it *is* the person. The person does not merely *have* a
body, it *is* a body, even though the person as such infinitely transcends
bodily limits. This is why everything that involves the body involves
the person as a whole. By refusing to consider the spiritual dimension
of human persons when we seek to alleviate their physical ailments,
we do them immeasurable harm. All too often we thereby deprive
ourselves from the outset of any real possibility of enabling them to
assume their condition profitably and to surmount the various trials
they have to face.

scan of bk

     In the following pages we are concerned to set forth, in a synthe-
sis that has not previously been made, the bases of a Christian theology of illness and suffering, and with it to consider various modes of
healing, together with the question of health as such. To do so, we rely
essentially on the foundational teachings of Holy Scripture and the
Church Fathers.

     Thereby we wish to open or to recall various perspectives that
might help people of our day understand the phenomenon of illness
and the diverse forms of suffering connected with it. And we want to
treat as well the question of various therapies, together with the mat-
ters of healing and health itself, and to do so in a framework larger
than the one usually provided by our civilization which is so dominated by values that are purely technological and material. This
approach, we would hope, will enable the reader better to assume the

burdens of illness and suffering. Above all, we hope to aid Christians better to situate these crucial experiences in the framework of their relationship with God, which, as with all human realities, is their only proper place.

I.

The Origins of Illness

THE ORIGINAL "PERFECTION"

Although he is the "Creator of all things visible and invisible," God cannot be considered to be the author of illness, suffering and death. The Fathers affirm this unanimously. In his homily entitled "God is not the cause of suffering," St Basil declares: "It is folly to believe that God is the author of our sufferings; this blasphemy [. . .] destroys God's goodness."[1] "Illness is not [. . .] fashioned by the hand of God."[2] "God, who made the body, did not make illness, just as he made the soul but by no means made sin."[3] It is equally clear that "God did not make death."[4] To those who object to the biblical affirmation that man is created in the image of God because of our mortal destiny, the short length our life, the painful character of the human condition, and our tendency to suffer all sorts of physical and mental illnesses, St Gregory of Nyssa replies: "The abnormal nature of the present conditions of human life are not enough to prove that man has never been in possession of goods [deriving from the image of God]. In fact, since man is the work of God, who was inspired by his goodness to give man life, no one can reasonably conclude that the creature who owes his existence to this goodness could have been plunged into suffering by his Creator. There is another cause for our present condition and for the factors that have deprived us of a more

---

[1] *Homily: God is not the cause of evil* 2; PG 31.332B.
[2] Ibid., 6.344A.
[3] Ibid., 6.344B.
[4] Ibid., 7.345A.

enviable state of being."⁵ "Only the most narrow-minded will appeal
to bodily sufferings, which inevitably mark the inconsistent character
of our [present] nature, as reason for naming God the author of our
ills, or will absolutely refuse God the title of man's Creator in order
to avoid imputing to God responsibility for our suffering."⁶ St Maximus the Confessor stresses that "God, in creating human nature, did
not introduce [. . .] suffering into it,"⁷ and that the susceptibility to
suffering, corruption and death that followed did not come from
God.⁸ For his part, St Gregory Palamas declares that "God created
neither death, nor illnesses, nor infirmities";⁹ "God created neither
the death of the soul nor the death of the body";¹⁰ "This death of the
body was not given by God; he neither made it nor did he ordain that
it should be.¹¹ [. . .] Nor is God the author of bodily illnesses."¹² The
author of the Book of Wisdom had already affirmed that "God did
not make death, and he does not delight in the death of the living.
For he created all things that they might exist, and the creatures of
the world are wholesome, and there is no destructive poison in them"
(Wis 1:13-14).

The inspired author of the Book of Genesis reveals that God's
creation at its beginning was wholly good (cf. Gen 1:31), and the
Fathers are unanimous in teaching that man himself, in the primordial state of his nature, knew nothing of illness, infirmity, suffering or
corruption.¹³ St Dorotheus of Gaza notes that "Man dwelt in the
delights of paradise [. . .], where he possessed the full range of his

---

⁵*Catechetical Discourse* V.8-9. See also ibid., 11 and VII.4. *Treatise on Virginity*,
XII.2.
⁶*Id.*, VIII.15.
⁷*To Thalassios* 61; PG 90.628A.
⁸Ibid., 41; PG 90.408C.
⁹*Homily* XXXI; PG 151.396B. Cf. 388D.
¹⁰*Theological and Ethical Chapters*, 51.
¹¹Cf. Ibid., 47.
¹²*Homily* XXXI; PG 151.396C; Cf. 388B.
¹³The term "corruption" (*phtora*) which we shall have reason to evoke throughout this book, possesses two distinct meanings: on the one hand, it designates the
dissolution of the body after death; on the other, any kind of alteration of the body
(and, in a broader sense, of the soul). This second meaning can refer to illnesses, suffering, fatigue, and the like. See St John of Damascus, *The Orthodox Faith* III.28.

faculties, being in the natural state in which he was created."[14]
According to St Augustine, man knew "in his flesh a perfect state of
health."[15] And St John Chrysostom adds: "If you wish to know the
state of our body as it left the hands of God, return to paradise,
and behold the man whom God had just placed there. His body was
not subject to corruption. Like a statue taken from the kiln, that
shines most brightly, he experienced none of the infirmities that
we know in our day."[16] St Gregory of Nyssa remarks that "neither illness nor deformity existed in the beginning with our [original]
nature"[17]; physical suffering, "the testings of the body that make
up part of our condition, our numerous illnesses: humanity at the
beginning knew none of these."[18] "Man at his origin," Gregory adds,
"did not possess the capacity to suffer, either by nature or as an
essential property associated with his nature; it is only later that the
capacity for suffering infected his nature."[19] The absence of suffering
and the condition of incorruptibility figure among the many qualities
that man, at the beginning, held in his possession.[20] "He who speaks
of the trials of the body which are a part of our human condition—
the numerous maladies that at its origin humanity did not know—
will shed abundant tears when he compares the [original] happiness
with his [present] suffering, the evils [he endures today] with the
blessings [he possessed in the beginning]."[21] St Maximus the Confessor writes: "The first man, receiving his being from God, came into
existence free of sin and corruption, for neither sin nor corruption
were created with him;"[22] and "the change in man toward suffering,

---

[14]*Instructions* I.1. Cf. Abba Isaiah, *Ascetic Writings* II.2.

[15]*The City of God* XIV.26.

[16]*Homilies on the Statutes* XI,2. Cf. *Homilies on Genesis* V.1 and 4: "Although
clothed with a body, man did not suffer at all from life's hard necessities." And XVI,1:
Adam and Eve, "although clothed with a body, did not experience infirmity. [. . .]
Their life was free of all pain and sadness." And XVI.4: They were "clothed with a
body without experiencing its weaknesses."

[17]*Letters* III.17.

[18]*Homilies on the Beatitudes* III.5. Cf. *Catechetical Discourse* V.8.

[19]*On Virginity* XII.2.

[20]*Homilies on the Beatitudes* III.5.

[21]Ibid.

[22]*To Thalassios* 21; PG 90.312B.

corruption and death was not there in the beginning."[23]

This double affirmation, that God did not create death and that man in his primordial condition was incorruptible, implies logically that man in the original state of his nature was also immortal. A number of patristic texts support this point.[24]

But a closer look reveals the fact that the Fathers' opinion in this regard was highly nuanced. Basing their reflection on the scriptural affirmation that "God fashioned man from the dust of the earth" (Gen 2:7), a number of them, concerned to preserve a clear distinction between the created and the uncreated, did not hesitate to insist that the human body at its creation and according to its very nature was unstable, corruptible and mortal. "Man was mortal by the very nature of his body," affirmed St Augustine.[25] St Athanasius adds: "By nature, man is mortal, since he is created from nothing."[26] And he affirms as well that at their origin men "were endowed with a corruptible nature."[27] St John Chrysostom notes that in paradise, although man did not experience any pressing need, he was "clothed in a mortal body."[28] The Fathers often nuance their affirmations by saying that man was created "for incorruptibility,"[29] or "for

---

[23]Ibid., 42; PG 90.408C.

[24]See St Athanasius of Alexandria, *Against the Pagans* 2-3; St Basil, *Homily: God is not the cause of evil* 7, PG 31.344C (God had granted Adam the "joy of eternal life"). Cf. St Gregory of Nyssa, *Cat. disc.* V.6 ("Since eternity was also one of the advantages stemming from the divine nature, it was absolutely necessary that the organization of our nature in this regard be such as to possess in itself the principle of immortality [*to athanaton*]"); ibid., V.8 (eternity is placed, together with the absence of physical suffering, among the attributes which Adam originally possessed); ibid., VIII.4-5 (the condition of mortality was originally reserved for irrational creatures); *On Virginity* XII.2 ("Man did not possess by himself, as an essential property of his nature, the capacity to die"). See as well St John of Damascus, *On the Orthodox Faith* II.12 ("God made man [. . .] immortal"); and St John Chrysostom, *Homilies on the Statutes* XI,2 (in paradise, the body "was not subject to death").

[25]*De Genesi ad litteram* VI.25; PL 34.345.

[26]*On the Incarnation of the Word* IV.6. Cf. IV.4.

[27]Ibid., V.1.

[28]*Homilies on Genesis* XVII.7.

[29]This is the expression found in Wis 2:23, quoted by St Athanasius, *On the Incarnation of the Word* V.2.

immortality,"[30] or that man's nature strives to participate in divine immortality,[31] or they speak of the "promise" of incorruptibility and immortality,[32] indicating that these values were not definitively acquired from the very beginning as they would have been if they were properties of human nature itself.

This means that the incorruptibility and immortality of the first man were due solely to divine grace. Immediately after creating man from the dust of the ground, Genesis affirms (2:7), God "breathed into him the breath of life, and man became a living being." The Fathers saw in this breath the human soul as well as the divine Spirit.[33] Because Adam's soul and body were penetrated with divine energies, they possessed supernatural qualities. Accordingly, St Gregory Palamas notes that divine grace "made up by a great number of blessings the insufficiencies of our nature."[34] It is by this grace that the body and soul could be perfectly healthy. "We were preserved from illness," St Basil remarks, "thanks to the gifts received at our creation."[35] And it is by this same grace that the body was rendered incorruptible and immortal.[36] Thus St Augustine notes that man "was mortal according to the nature of his body, but immortal by grace."[37] St Athanasius speaks of man living an "immortal life" in that he "possessed the gifts of God and the special power that came to him from the Father's Word."[38] And he notes as well "men were of a corruptible nature, but by the grace of participation in the Word" they

---

[30]St Gregory of Nyssa, *Catechetical Discourse* VIII.5; *Hom. on the Beatitudes* III.5.

[31]Cf. St Gregory of Nyssa, *Catechetical Discourse* V.6; St Athanasius, *Against the Pagans* 2; St Gregory Palamas, *Theological and Ethical Chapters* 47.

[32]Cf. St Athanasius, *On the Incarnation of the Word* III.4. St Maximus, *Ambigua* 10; PG 91.1156D.

[33]See, for example, St Gregory Palamas, *Homilies* LVII, ed. S. Oikonomos, *Gregoriou tou Palama omiliai* (Athens, 1861), p. 213.

[34]*Homilies* XXXVI; PG 151.452A.

[35]Longer Rule, 55.

[36]Cf. St Basil's homily, *God is not the cause of evil* 7, PG 31.344C; St Maximus *Commentary on the Lord's Prayer*, PG 90.904C; *Ad Thalassios*, Introduction, PG 90.252D; St Gregory Palamas, *Theological and Ethical Chapters* 46; *Homily* XXXVI; PG 151.452A; *Homily* LIV, ed. Oikonomos, p. 213.

[37]*De Genesi ad litteram* VI.25; PL 34.354.

[38]Against the Pagans 2.

could "escape this condition of their nature"[39] since, "because of the Word present with them, the corruption of their nature could not approach them."[40]

Because of this grace, Adam found himself in a condition very different not only from that of other beings living in nature,[41] but also from the human condition that we presently know.[42] It is this privileged, superior condition that we call "paradise."[43] To indicate this access by grace to a superior condition, the Fathers comment on the text of Gen. 2:8 by affirming that man was not created in paradise but was placed there by God,[44] and thereby they draw a clear distinction between paradise and the rest of the earth.[45] This condition concerned not only the soul, but also the body.[46] St Maximus thus speaks of the "difference in the constitution of the human body before the fall in the case of our father Adam, and that which now holds us in its power."[47] Although they remark that it is scarcely possible for us to conceive of this condition from the perspective of our present fallen state,[48] the Fathers imagine that this primal condition was similar to that of the angels.[49] According to St Gregory of Nyssa and St Maximus in particular, the body of the first Adam did not possess the materiality and heaviness that now characterize human bodies.[50] His

---

[39] *On the Incarnation of the Word* V.1.

[40] Ibid., V.2.

[41] Cf. St John of Damascus, *The Orthodox Faith* II.11, 30; St John Chrysostom, *Homilies on Genesis* XVI.1; St Gregory of Nyssa, *Catechetical Disc.* VIII.4.

[42] Cf. St Gregory of Nyssa, *Catechetical Discourse* V.9.

[43] Cf. St John of Damascus, *The Orthodox Faith* II.11.

[44] Cf. St Theophilus of Antioch: "God transported [man] from the earth, of which he was made, to paradise" (*To Autolycus* II.24); St John Chrysostom: "God created man outside of paradise, but he placed him there immediately" (*Homilies on Genesis* XIII.4).

[45] See, for example, St Maximus, *Ambigua* 41; PG 91.1305A &D.

[46] Cf. St John of Damascus, *The Orthodox Faith* II.11.

[47] Cf. *Ambigua* 45; PG 91.1353A.

[48] Cf. St Gregory of Nyssa, *Catechetical Discourse* V.9.

[49] Cf. St John Chrysostom, *Homilies on Genesis* XVI.1.

[50] St Maximus, *Ambigua* 45; PG 91.1353AB: "The first man was naked, not in that he possessed neither flesh nor body, but in that he did not possess this material constitution that renders flesh both mortal and hard." For the thought of St Gregory

nature was rather that of the resurrected body described by St Paul in
I Corinthians 15; and it should be noted in this sense that the Fathers
see in the state following the resurrection a reintegration into paradise.[51]

However, since man was created with freedom, whether or not he
preserved this state of grace depended on his free will. It was his
responsibility to remain in a condition of incorruption and immortality which grace bestowed upon him, or, to the contrary, to lose it

---

of Nyssa on the subject, see J. Daniélou, *Platonisme et théologie mystique. Doctrine
spirituelle de saint Grégoire de Nysse* (Paris, 1944), pp. 56-59.

[51]Cf. St Theophilus of Antioch, *To Autolycus* II.26; St Basil, *On the Origin of
Man* II.7; St Gregory of Nyssa, *On the Creation of Man* XVII; PG 44.188CD; XXI,
204A; St Maximus the Confessor, *To Thalassios* 61.669A. The Fathers have radically
different conceptions of the origin of man than those held by modern science. The
history of man as it is conceived by human paleontology, as compared with the point
of view of Holy Tradition, refers only to the history of humanity outside of paradise.
The Fathers would see *homo habilis* not as a representative of humanity as he
emerged from the hands of God, but as already fallen from his original state, fallen
to the lowest state of his "involution," and beginning to develop himself according to
a new mode of existence. (It is important, therefore, to avoid confusing the state of
spiritual infancy attributed by the Fathers to Adam at the time of his creation [Cf.
St Irenaeus, *Against Heresies* IV.38.1; St Theophilus of Antioch, *To Autolycus* II.25; St
John of Damascus, *The Orthodox Faith* II.11] with the historical "infancy" or a state
of underdevelopment that characterized the earliest human beings.) The original
condition of man as it is presented by Scripture and the Fathers is situated in another
temporal order than that of historical knowledge: it does not belong to the time of
sensible realities (*chronos*), but to the duration of spiritual realities (*aiōn*), which
eludes historical science because it belongs to the sphere of spiritual history. Without being "non-temporal" (because it had a beginning in time and developed over
time, which it in fact began), the existence of Adam in his primitive state is "ante-
historical," just as human existence following the parousia will be post-historical.
Spiritual history, then, cannot be replaced by historical science. The teaching of Tradition about human origins is neither more nor less incompatible with our present
knowledge of human paleontology than is the faith of the Church in the eucharistic
transformation of bread and wine into Body and Blood of Christ with the findings
of the science of chemistry, or faith in the Ascension of Christ with the findings of
physics and astronomy. In each of these cases, we are dealing with two different
modes of apprehension that cannot be reduced one to another. Each concerns different modes of being and of becoming. Faith and spiritual knowledge correspond to
a domain in which the laws of nature are transcended and to a mode of existence that
is, in the proper sense of the term, "super-natural."

by rejecting that grace.[52] Thus, when the Fathers affirm that man was created incorruptible and immortal, they do not mean that he could not become corrupt and die, but that he had by grace and free choice the possibility not to corrupt himself and die. In order for his incorruptibility and immortality to be preserved and become permanent aspects of his being, man had to preserve the grace which God had given to him, and remain united to God through the aid of the commandment issued for this purpose (cf. Gen 2:16-17[53]).[54] In the words of St Gregory Palamas: "At the beginning, man was not only a creature of God, he was also His son in the Spirit. This grace was accorded him together with his soul, through the vivifying Breath (cf. Gen 2:7). It served as a foretaste [of the coming Kingdom]: if man had observed the commandment and benefited from this foretaste, he would have enjoyed through it a still more perfect union with God; he would have become co-eternal with God, clothed with immortality."[55]

We can well understand, then, why the Fathers often say that man, in the beginning and until the first sin, was in fact neither mortal nor immortal. St Theophilus of Antioch writes: "Yet someone will say to us, 'But wasn't death a natural function of human nature?' Not at all! 'Was man therefore immortal?' We do not say that either. They will then reply, 'Do you mean man was nothing at all?' No, that is not at all what we mean. Rather, by his nature man was no more mortal than immortal. If he had been created immortal from the beginning, he would have been created divine. On the other hand, if he had been created mortal, it would have appeared that God was the cause of his

---

[52]Cf. St Athanasius, *On the Incarnation of the Word* III.4; St Maximus, *To Thalassios* 61; PG 90.632B; St John of Damascus, *The Orthodox Faith* II.30.

[53]Cf. Wis 6:18: "Obedience to God's laws guarantees incorruptibility."

[54]The Fathers in this regard stress the responsibility of man dependent on his free will (which determines his voluntary relationship to God), as much as they do the concern of God, who desires not man's death but his immortality. See St Athanasius, *On the Incarnation of the Word* III.4-5; IV.4; St John Chrysostom, *Homilies on Genesis* XVII.3; St Gregory Palamas, *Theological and Ethical Chapters* 47 and *Homilies* XXXI; PG 151.388D.

[55]*Homilies* LVII, ed. Oikonomos, p. 213. Cf. St John of Damascus, *The Orthodox Faith* II.11.

death. Thus he was created neither mortal nor immortal; rather, he was capable of both mortality and immortality. Had he chosen the way of immortality in following the divine commandment, he would have received the gift of immortality as a recompense, and thus he would have become like God. Since instead he turned toward works of death in disobedience to God, he became himself the cause of his own death. So it is that God created man free and master of his own destiny."[56]

St Augustine adds in this regard: "Until sin entered in, the human body could be qualified in one sense as mortal and in another sense as immortal; mortal because it was capable of dying, and immortal because it could have not died. [. . .] By refraining from sin, it could have avoided death."[57] And St Athanasius notes in the same vein: "Knowing that man's free will could have inclined him to one choice or the other, God took the initiative and strengthened the grace that He had given man by providing him with the commandment already in the Garden. In that way, insofar as man preserved that grace and dwelt in virtue, he would know in Paradise a life free of sadness, pain and anxiety, together with the promise of immortality in heaven. But if man transgressed that commandment, he would know that in death he would experience the corruption of his nature, and that he would no longer live in Paradise but would have been expelled, to die and to dwell henceforth in death and corruption."[58] St Gregory Palamas even sees in the divine commandment a means given by God to man by which he could avoid corruption and death while preserving his freedom,[59] and he stresses that immortality and death, incorruptibility and corruption, depended in fact on man's choice,[60] since God,

---

[56] *To Autolycus* II.27. Cf. I.24, "Man was created in an intermediate situation, neither completely mortal nor absolutely immortal, but capable of both."

[57] *De Genesi ad litteram* VI.25; PG 34.354.

[58] *On the Incarnation of the Word* III.4. Cf. St John of Damascus The Orthodox Faith II.30.

[59] *Homilies* XXXI; PG 151.388D. Cf. *Homilies* LIV, ed. Oikonomos, p. 213; *Theological and Ethical Chapters* 51.

[60] *Homilies* XXXI; PG 151.388D; and XXIX; PG 151.369C. Cf. St John Chrysostom, *Homilies on Genesis* XVII.7.

having created man free, could not prevent him from choosing what he would do and what he would become.[61]

THE INITIAL CAUSE OF ILLNESS: ORIGINAL SIN

According to the Fathers, then, we need to seek the source of illness,[62] infirmities, sufferings,[63] corruption,[64] and death,[65] together with all other evils that presently afflict human nature, in the personal will of man,[66] in the bad use to which he has put his free will, that is, in the sin which he committed in Paradise. As St Maximus the Confessor affirms: "The misuse of his freedom of choice introduced into Adam susceptibility to punishment, corruptibility and mortality."[67] St Theophilus of Antioch notes: "For the first creature, disobedience procured exclusion from Paradise; [. . .] in his disobedience, man

---

[61] *Homilies* XXXI; PG 151.388D.

[62] Cf. St Irenaeus, *Against Heresies* V.15.2. St Gregory of Nyssa, *On the Soul and the Resurrection*; PG 46.149A. St John Chrysostom, *Homilies on Genesis* XVII.7.

[63] Cf. St Maximus, *To Thalassios* 61; PG 90.628BC, 629D, 632B; *Chapters on theology and economy* III.18. St John of Damascus, *The Orthodox Faith* II.30. St Gregory Palamas, *To the Nun Xenia*; PG 150.1048C.

[64] Cf. St Athanasius, *On the Incarnation of the Word* III.4-5; IV.4; V.1-3. St Gregory of Nyssa, *On the Creation of Man* XX; PG 44.200C. St Maximus the Confessor, *Commentary on the Lord's Prayer*; PG 90.904C; *To Thalassios* 61, PG 90.636A; *Ambigua* 10, PG 91.1156D; *Letters* X, PG 91.449B. St John of Damascus, *The Orthodox Faith* II.30; III.1. St Gregory Palamas, *To the Nun Xenia*; PG 150.1048C.

[65] Cf. Rom 5:12. *To Diogenetes* XII.2. St Justin, *Dialog* 124. St Irenaeus, *Against Heresies* IV.38.4. St Athanasius, *On the Incarnation of the Word* III.4-5; IV.4; V.1-3. St Basil *Homily: God is not the cause of evil* 7. St Gregory of Nyssa, *Catechetical Discourse* VIII.4; *On the Creation of Man* XX, PG 44.200C; *On Virginity* XII.2; *On the Soul and the Resurrection*, PG 46.149A. St John Chrysostom, *Homilies on Genesis*, XVII.7. St Maximus, *Ambigua* 7 and 10, PG 91.1093A and 1156D; *To Thalassios* 61, PG 90.629B&D, 632B, 633BC, 636B. St John of Damascus, *The Orthodox Faith* II.30 and III.1. St Gregory Palamas, *To the Nun Xenia*, PG 150.1048C; *Theological and Ethical Chapters* 46, 50, 51; *Homilies* XI, PG 151.125A.

[66] See, for ex., St John Chrysostom, *Homilies on Genesis* XVI.1.5, 6; XVII.7. St Gregory of Nyssa, *Catechetical Discourse*, V.11, VII.1; *On the Creation of Man* XX, PG 44.201A; *On Virginity* XII.2. St Maximus *To Thalassios* 42, PG 90.408BC; *Letters* X, PG 91.449B. St John of Damascus, *The Orthodox Faith* III.1.

[67] *To Thalassios* 42, PG 90.408B.

acquired fatigue, suffering and distress, and finally he fell into the power of death."[68] It is "because of the sin of disobedience that illnesses torment mankind," St Irenaeus declares.[69] And similarly, St Nil Sorsky says: "After transgressing the commandment, Adam was subject to illness."[70] The same thought is developed more explicitly by St Gregory Palamas: "From where do we get our weaknesses, illnesses and other evils that give rise to death? From where does death itself come? From our disobedience to the divine commandment, from transgression of the precept which God gave to us, from our original sin in the Paradise of God. Thus sicknesses, infirmities and the weight of all sorts of trials are the result of sin. Because of sin, in fact, we have clothed our sick bodies in garments of skin; mortal and overwhelmed with suffering, we pass through this temporary, impermanent world, and we have been condemned to live our lives at the mercy of countless evils and multitudes of calamities. Illness, as a result, is like a short and difficult pathway down which sin has led the human race, and the end of this pathway, its ultimate limit, is death."[71]

By choosing to follow the Devil's suggestion to become "like gods" (Gen 3:5)—that is, to become gods apart from God[72]—Adam and Eve deprived themselves of grace, and from that time on they lost the qualities that would have bestowed on them in some manner a supernatural condition.[73] St Athanasius affirms, "The transgression

---

[68] *To Autolycus* II.25.

[69] *Against Heresies* V.15.2.

[70] *Rule* VII.

[71] *Homilies* XXXI, PG 151.388BC. The same teaching appears in St John Chrysostom, *Homilies on the Statutes* XI.2, and St Theophilus of Antioch, *To Autolycus* II.25.

[72] According to many Fathers, the original sin consisted of an attempt on man's part to become self-deifying. See, for example, St John Chrysostom, *Homilies on the Statutes* XI.2; St Irenaeus, *Against Heresies* V.3.1; St John of Damascus, *The Orthodox Faith* II.30; St Symeon the New Theologian, *Ethical Treatises* XIII.60. That man was destined to become god is affirmed only by the Eastern Fathers (see J. Gross, *La Divinisation du chrétien d'après les Pères grecs*, Paris 1938), but this deification occurs only in God and by Him.

[73] Cf. St Gregory of Nyssa, *Catechetical Discourse* V.11. St John of Damascus, *The Orthodox Faith* II.30. St John Chrysostom, *Homilies on Genesis* XVI.4. St Gregory Palamas, *Theological and Ethical Chapters* 46, 48, 66.

of the commandment brought them back to their own nature,"[74] that is, to the dust of the earth from which they were formed,[75] (Gen 2:7), according to God's word to Adam, "You will return to the earth from which you were taken; for you are dust, and to dust you shall return" (Gen 3:19). The evils that Adam and Eve endured following their sin were a natural consequence of their voluntary rejection of communion with God which enabled them to participate in God's properties. By separating themselves from the Good, they exposed human nature to all kinds of evil.[76] St Gregory of Nyssa writes: "This rejection of the Good, once accomplished, had as a consequence the appearance of all forms of evil: the fact that man turned away from life led to death; by depriving himself of the light, he fell into darkness; lacking virtue, evil appeared in his life; and thus it is that all forms of good were one by one replaced by a series of opposite evils."[77] St Gregory notes as well: "Having by trickery mingled vice with man's free will, the Enemy managed to eliminate and obscure the divine blessing. With this blessing lacking, its very opposite necessarily appeared in its place. Thus death opposes life, weakness opposes strength, etc."[78]

These ills affected first of all the human soul, exposing it to punishment, sadness and suffering. The soul became corrupted and subject to death, separated as it was from God and deprived of divine life.[79] Then the soul transmitted these ills to man's body. This double

---

[74]*On the Incarnation of the Word* IV.4.

[75]Cf. ibid., 5.

[76]Recall that, according to the majority of Greek Fathers, in the first place evil only exists through the personal will of demons or of man, and in the second place it has no positive essence since it is only the negation of the good. On this issue, see Dionysius the Areopagite, *Divine Names* V.19-35; PG 3.716D-736B.

[77]Catechetical Discourse VIII.19.

[78]Ibid. V.11. Cf. St Basil, *Homily: God is not the cause of evil* 7: "Death is a necessary consequence of sin; one draws near to death to the degree that one distances oneself from life, which is God. Death is the absence of life: by distancing himself from God, Adam exposed himself to death." St Maximus, *Ambigua* 10; PG 91.1156D: "The first man, because he refused to nourish himself [of the Word of life], inevitably distanced himself from divine life, and in return another sort of life became his, one that engendered death since it was lacking the Word."

[79]Cf. St John Chrysostom, *Homilies on the Statutes* XI.2. St Gregory Palamas, *To*

death, both spiritual and bodily,[80] is signified, according to St Athanasius, by the insistence of the formula the Book of Genesis attributes to God in His warning to Adam and Eve (Gen 2:17): "The day in which you eat [of the tree of the knowledge of good and evil], you will surely die" (literally, "you will die of death").[81] In the same way, St Gregory Palamas stipulates: "Death entering into the soul by way of the transgression not only corrupts the soul itself, it also afflicts the body with pains and passions, rendering it corruptible and in the end subjecting it to death. Therefore, following the death of the inner man through the transgression, the earthly Adam heard, 'You are dust and to dust you shall return.' (Gen 3:19)."[82]

Thus it occurred that, ceasing by Adam's transgression to conform itself to God, human nature in its entirety "fell sick with corruption."[83] It lost the exceptional condition which it possessed from the beginning by virtue of indwelling grace,[84] and as a result it fell into "an inferior condition."[85] St Athanasius notes: "Men no longer remained as they had begun to be."[86] Whereas the original mode of his existence drew man close to the angelic state, his new condition drew him rather toward an animal-like existence.[87] His body

---

the Nun Xenia, PG 150.1048C; *Homilies* XI, PG 151,125A. This spiritual death, which Gregory Palamas defines as the separation of the soul from God—whereas physical death is the separation of the soul from the body—is more serious than its physical counterpart and constitutes true death (*To Xenia*, loc. cit.).

[80]This double death is clearly what St Paul envisaged as he affirmed, in Rom 5:12, that "by one man sin entered into the world, and by sin, death"; and in 1 Cor 15:21, that "death came by a single man."

[81]*On the Incarnation of the Word* III.5.

[82]*To the Nun Xenia*, PG 150.1048C. Cf. *Theological and Ethical Chapters* 51.

[83]St Cyril of Alexandria, *Commentary on Romans*, PG 74,789B.

[84]The link between cause and effect affirmed by Holy Tradition between spiritual death and physical death—a link hardly comprehensible if one envisages it directly and on a purely natural level—becomes clear in the light of the mediation of grace: spiritual death implies loss of that grace which confers upon the body both incorruption and immortality.

[85]St Gregory of Nyssa, *Catechetical Discourse* V.11.

[86]*On the Incarnation of the Word* IV.4.

[87]Cf. St Maximus, *Ambigua* 42; PG 91.1348A. St Gregory of Nyssa, *On the Soul and the Resurrection*, PG 46.148C. On this last passage, see J. Daniélou, *Platonisme et théologie mystique*, pp. 56-59.

acquired a material dimension,[88] a heaviness[89] and opaqueness[90] which it did not know at its origin. It entered into the flow of sensible animal life, and henceforth it is subjected to the movements, the instability and the divisions that other natural beings know and from which it formerly remained free by virtue of grace. This new condition of existence is signified in the Book of Genesis by the expression "garments of skin" (Gen 3:21).[91] These garments of skin symbolize both the material, animal, mortal aspect of human life, and the fact that this condition is *added* to man's true nature.[92]

Commenting on a passage of St Gregory of Nazianzus which evokes Adam's original nudity, St Maximus writes: "I suspect that this is the difference between the constitution of the human body before the fall with regard to our father Adam, and that which now holds us in bondage . . . In the beginning, man was not torn between opposed qualities that wreaked mutual injury on each other in his human constitution. No, he remained free of the movement of such qualities, free of their perpetual change and of their mutual domination. It was as if by grace he continued to be incorruptible, without being tortured by their pricks, having an entirely different constitution, one in harmony with his body, characterized by simplicity and peace. The first man was naked, not in the sense that he possessed neither flesh nor body, but in that he was free of that more material constitution that renders the flesh mortal and hard."[93]

The "very grave illness" that affects man reaches through him to the entire cosmos.[94] St Maximus explains: "Receiving by the grace of

---

[88]Cf. St Maximus, *Ambigua* 45; PG91.1353B.

[89]Cf. St John of Damascus, *The Orthodox Faith* III.1. St Maximus, *Ambigua* 45; PG 91.1353B.

[90]Cf. St John of Damascus, *The Orthodox Faith* III.1.

[91]V. Lossky notes: "The garments of skin represent our present nature, our common biological state, very different from the transparent corporality of Paradise." See his "Theologie dogmatique" in *Messager de l'exarchat du Patriarche russe en Europe occidentale* 48, 1964, p. 231.

[92]Cf. St Gregory of Nyssa, *On the Soul and the Resurrection*; PG 46.148C-149A.

[93]*Ambigua* 45; PG 91.1353AB.

[94]Cf. St John of Damascus, *The Orthodox Faith* II.30. See as well, V. Lossky, *Mystical Theology of the Eastern Church* (New York: SVS Press, 1991), pp. 132-133; "Théologie Dogmatique," p. 227.

God his Creator the vocation to serve as master of the whole world, man misused this vocation by turning his activity against nature; thereby he introduced into nature—and into the cosmos as a whole—the change for the worse that characterizes its present state."[95]

God created the world "good" (Gen 1:31), but it was man's responsibility to preserve it as such. God created man as a microcosm within the macrocosm,[96] so that man might recapitulate every created being.[97] God established man as king of the creation (cf. Gen 1:28-30), granting him power over all things within it.[98] He made him mediator between Himself and His creatures,[99] giving man the task of leading created beings to their perfection by uniting them with God through participation in the grace which he received from the Spirit.[100] According to St Maximus, man's primary mission was to unite Paradise with the rest of the earth, and thereby to enable all other created beings to participate in the conditions of Paradise.[101] Thus Adam was to enable all other creatures to participate in the order, harmony and peace of which his own nature benefited because of its union with God, and this included the incorruptibility and immortality he received by grace.[102]

But once Adam turned away from God, nature was no longer subject to him. Following Adam's sin, disorder established itself between the beings of creation as it did within man himself. "Cursed is the ground because of you!" (Gen 3:17), God declares to man, thus announcing the cosmic catastrophe which his sin had provoked. The distinction and separation that naturally characterized created beings

---

[95]*Letters* X; PG 91.449B.
[96]Cf. St John of Damascus, *The Orthodox Faith* II.12. St Maximus, *Mystagogy* VII.
[97]St Gregory Palamas, *Homilies* LIII.
[98]Cf. St Gregory of Nyssa, *On the Creation of Man* IV; PG 44.136C; *Catechical Discourse* VI.10.
[99]Cf. St Maximus, *Ambigua* 41; PG 91.1305A-C. St John of Damascus, *The Orthodox Faith* II.30.
[100]See St Maximus, *Ambigua* 41; PG 91.1305A-C.
[101]See ibid., 1305D.
[102]St Maximus thus speaks of a deification of all creatures as the ultimate purpose of creation.

now became opposition and division. Man, now deprived of the grace that constituted his protection (cf. Gen 3:7)[103] and having lost his power over nature, became weak in the face of nature and subject to its negative effects.

Evil spread all the more rapidly and actively as the Devil, whom Adam obeyed, seized power over man, usurping the privileges that God had accorded Adam when He established him as master of the other creatures. With regard to dominion over nature, the "Prince of this world" replaced the "King of Creation." Sickness thus appeared as an effect of Adam's sin; it was the consequence and form of evil his sin engendered. Illness multiplied, grew, spread and reinforced itself. Occasionally it became "incarnated" by the "powers of darkness and malice," the Devil and the demons, who thus became one of the chief sources of illness. Most often they manifested themselves indirectly by way of illness. But at times they appeared directly, without mediation, as in cases of possession where they occupied in man the vacuum that should have been filled by God.[104] God, who envisions the salvation of man and through man of the entire universe,[105] does not allow the forces of evil to submerge and destroy His creation. Man

---

[103]Cf. St John Chrysostom, *Homilies on Genesis* XVI.5.

[104]The demonic etiology of certain illnesses is affirmed by the Scriptures: explicitly in the prologue to the Book of Job (Job 2:6-7), and implicitly in the words of the Apostle Peter, "God anointed Jesus of Nazareth with the Holy Spirit and with power; . . . he went about doing good and healing all that were oppressed by the devil, for God was with him" (Acts 10:38). In addition, there are numerous biblical accounts of miracles where the demonic origin of illness clearly appears. The Fathers also affirm such an etiology. See esp. *Apophthegmata* (alph. series), Theodora 3; St Gregory of Nyssa (see A.M. Keenan, "St Gregory of Nyssa and the Medical Profession," *Bulletin of the History of Medicine* 15, 1944, pp. 159-160); St Barsanuphius, *Letters* 154, 517, 519, 520, 521; *Life of St Theodore of Sykeon*: 43, 46, 71, 84, 86, 88, 89, 91, 106, 108, 140, 143; St Maximus the Confessor, *Centuries on love* II, 74; St Elias Ecdicos, *Anthology* 49; St Symeon Metaphrastis, *Paraphrase of the Homilies of St Makarios of Egypt* 147 (*The Philokalia*, ed. G.E.H. Palmer, Philip Sherrard, Kallistos Ware, London: Faber, 1984, vol. III, p. 352). This recognition of a demonic etiology does not prevent the Fathers (as we shall see in Ch. 3) from admitting as well a biological, organic or functional etiology as parallel or secondary. Far from excluding physical causality, the "metaphysical" or spiritual origin of illness includes the physical aspect, recognizing it to be a necessary vehicle for manifesting the demonic.

[105]Cf. St Maximus, *To Thalassios* 60; PG 90.621AB.

image vs likeness

and nature remain partially protected by His Providence, which imposes certain limits on the negative activity of the Devil and his demons.[106] Thereby God stabilizes the cosmos in its slide toward nothingness, establishing a certain order in the very heart of disorder.[107] Even if man has lost the "likeness" of God which he began to acquire, he nevertheless remains bearer of the divine "image," even if that image is veiled, obscured and deformed.[108] Thus man is not totally deprived of grace. Even in his weakness he retains sufficient spiritual power to be able, if he wishes, to turn again toward God and to obey the commandments which he continues to receive from Him (Dt 30:11-19). And thereby he is able to maintain, according to God's own promise, a certain mastery over nature (cf. Gen 9:1-2).

man's ability

Nonetheless, this new balance remains fragile. Man and nature have become a battleground where evil and good, death and life, wage a permanent, merciless combat against each other. This combat is made evident by sickness, infirmity and suffering; and until the Incarnation of Christ, its outcome was uncertain.

Are People Responsible for the Illnesses That Afflict Them?

How then are we to answer the question of the relation between illness and sin, and of human responsibility in the appearance and development of the illnesses that afflict us? From what we have said, it appears clearly that this relation and this responsibility exist from the very beginning of the creation of man. For illness—even in the demonic activity that becomes manifest through it—is a direct consequence of the personal sin of Adam and Eve. Furthermore, the Fathers often depict illness, together with the other evils that result from the original sin, as a punishment.

---

[106]This appears clearly in the Prologue to the Book of Job.

[107]V. Lossky, "Théologie dogmatique," p. 27.

[108]Cf. St Gregory Palamas, *Theological and Ethical Chapters* 39; PG 151.1148B. Origen, *Homilies on Genesis* XIII.4. St John Chrysostom, *Exhortations to Theodore* I.3.

This notion of punishment, however, should not be understood in the sense of a punishment inflicted on man by a vengeful and cruel God. By committing sin, man himself engenders his own punishment. "He makes a pit, digging it out, and falls into the hole which he has made. His mischief returns upon his own head, and on his own pate his violence descends," declares the Psalmist (Ps 7:17-17). "Each of us chooses punishments when we sin willfully," writes Clement of Alexandria,[109] taking up a phrase of Plato, whom he quotes immediately afterwards: "It is the fault of him who made the choice; God is not responsible."[110] St Irenaeus writes in the same vein: "Upon all those who separate themselves from Him, God inflicts the separation that they themselves have chosen. Now separation from God is death; separation from the light is darkness; separation from God means the loss of all good things that come from Him. Therefore, those who, by their apostasy, have lost all these things plunge themselves into all sorts of punishments. Not that God takes the initiative in punishing them, but punishment follows by the very fact that they are deprived of every good."[111] When God specifies to our first parents the evils that will result from their transgression (Gen 3:16-19), He does not produce those evils; He merely predicts and describes them.

Because Adam is the "root" of human nature,[112] its prototype who embodies the very principle of all human existence,[113] he transmits his state to each of his descendants.[114] Death, corruption, illness and *inherited* suffering thus become the legacy of the entire human race.

Since this generation is perpetuated biologically from generation to generation,[115] everyone at his birth inherits Adam's fallen nature,

---

[109] *Pedagogue* I, VIII.69.1.

[110] *Republic* X.617e.

[111] *Against Heresies* V.27.2; cf. 28.1.

[112] Cf. St Mark the Hermit, *On the Hypostatic Union* 18. St Gregory Palamas, *Homilies* LII.

[113] Cf. St Gregory of Nyssa, *On the Creation of Man* XVI.185B and XXII.204CD. St Gregory Palamas, *Homilies* V; PG 151.64-65.

[114] Cf. St Maximus, *Ambigua* 10.1156D; *To Thalassios* 61; PG 90.628C, 632ABD, 633BC, 636AB.

[115] Cf. Theodoret of Cyrus, *Commentary on Romans*; PG 82.1245A. St Maximus, *To Thalassios* 21; PG 90.312C-313A; 61.628C, 632ABD. St John of Damascus, *The Orthodox Faith* II.30. St Gregory Palamas, *Homilies* V; PG 151.64B.

with its sickness and infirmity, marked by the consequences of his sin.[116] St Gregory of Nyssa explains: "It is as if human creatures, who in the beginning by their transgression welcomed sin and ushered in illness,[117] had woven evil into our very substance. Nature wills that every species of animal perpetuate itself by transmitting its heritage to its offspring. . . . In the same way, humans are born of humans, and in being born they bear human deficiencies."[118]

This state affects all men, even if they themselves have not personally sinned: "One man's trespass led to condemnation for all men" (Rom 5:18); "many died through one man's trespass" (Rom 5:15); and "death reigned [. . .] even over those whose sins were not like the transgression of Adam" (Rom 5:14), St Paul remarks. And he adds that "by one man's disobedience, many were made sinners" (Rom 5:19). That means, according to the Eastern Fathers, that men inherit not the sin of Adam itself, but rather its *consequences*.[119] St John Chrysostom comments on this passage: "The apostle affirms that many have become sinners because of the disobedience of a single man. That a man who sins and becomes mortal should pass on that mortality to his descendants is not at all improbable; but is it logical that one man should become a sinner because of the disobedience of another? It seems reasonable that no one should be punished for anything other than a personal sin. What indeed does the word "sinners" mean here? It means, I would say, 'subject to punishment and

---

[116]Cf. St Maximus, ibid.

[117]The term is used here in a general sense.

[118]*Homilies on the Beatitudes* VI.5. Cf. St Maximus, *To Thalassios* 61.632A. St Gregory Palamas, *Homilies* XLIII and LIV.

[119]We stipulate "the Eastern Fathers," since the Western line of thought, which has its source in the theology of St Augustine, diverges on this point by affirming the hereditary character of the sin of Adam itself, or at least of his guilt. On this divergence, see J. Meyendorff, "*Eph' ō* (Rom 5:12) chez Cyrille d'Alexandrie et Théodoret," *Studia Patristica* IV (1961), pp. 157-161, and his *Byzantine Theology* (New York: Fordham Univ. Press, 1974), pp. 143-146. See also the studies by S. Lyonnet, "Le sens de *Eph' ō* en Rom V, 12 et l'exégèse des Pères grecs," *Biblica* 36 (1955), pp. 436-456; "Le péché originel et l'exégèse de Rom V, 12-14," *Recherches de science religieuse* 44 (1956), pp. 63-84; "Péché originel," *Dictionnaire de la Bible*, Supplément 7 (1966), cols. 509-567.

Soup Support

condemned to death.'"[120] St Cyril of Alexandria expresses the same idea: "Nature fell ill from sin through the disobedience of a single man, Adam. Thereby the multitude of human beings was made sinful: not because they shared Adam's sin—they did not even exist yet; but because they shared his nature which had fallen under the law of sin."[121]

From this perspective, then, the illnesses that afflict human beings appear to be due not to their personal sins, but to the fact that they share in the fallen human nature of their first father Adam. Consequently, several passages of Scripture demonstrate that there exists no *a priori* link between a person's illness or infirmity and any specific sin or sins which that person or his or her immediate ancestors might have committed. Consider first of all the episode of the blind man in John 9:1-3. To His disciples' question, "Master, who sinned, this man or his parents, that he should have been born blind?", Jesus replied clearly: "Neither he nor his parents sinned." Then there is the account of the paralytic (Mt 9:1-6; Mk 2:1-2; Lk 5:17-26). Christ first says to him: "Your sins are forgiven," and it is by a second miracle that He heals his paralysis, ordering him to "Rise, take up your pallet and walk!" If his bodily infirmity had been the consequence of his sin, it would have been enough for Christ simply to forgive his sins, in order that the man be healed of his bodily illness at the same time as he received healing of his soul, without the need for a second intervention.

Note finally that St James, recommending that in cases of illness the elders of the Church be called to pray over the ill person and anoint him with oil, stipulates: "the prayer of faith will save the sick man, and the Lord will raise him up; and if he has committed sins, he will be forgiven" (Jas 5:14-15). Using the conditional ("and if"), St James indicates that there is no necessary link between the patient's

---

[120]*Homilies on Romans* X.2-3. St John Chrysostom states further (ibid., 1): "Adam, by eating the forbidden fruit, became the cause of the death of his descendants, even though they did not eat of the fruit of the tree"; and again, "that one man should be punished for another hardly seems just."

[121]*Commentary on Romans*, PG 74.789. We find a similar commentary in St Theophylact of Bulgaria, *Commentary on Romans*, PG 124.404C.

illness and the sins he might have committed. In addition to these, we could quote as well any number of Old Testament passages which depict the righteous afflicted with serious illnesses and bearing acute physical suffering. The most striking, of course, is the case of Job.

The fact that Adam is at the origin of the fall of human nature, however, does not mean that he alone is responsible for man's present state.[122] All men, in fact, bear responsibility to the degree that they have become imitators of Adam. It is because Adam's descendants have also committed sin that the consequences of Adam's sin have affected them. This is precisely St Paul's teaching: "by one man sin entered into the world, and by sin death; thus death spread to all men, because all men sinned" (Rom 5:12; cf. 3:23).[123]

St Cyril of Alexandria wrote on this subject: "The Serpent, who invented sin and in his perversity won a victory over Adam, thereby gained access to man's intelligence; for 'They have all gone astray, they are all alike corrupt' (Ps 13/14:3; Rom 3:12) [. . .] and death has swallowed us in its victory, according to the words of the prophet, 'Sheol has enlarged its appetite and opened its mouth beyond

---

[122]Adam's responsibility is first of all for his own sin and its consequences in his own life. Those consequences which affect his descendants result from the fact that Adam is the prototype of humanity and of the mode of generation by which humanity perpetuates itself as a result of his sin. From this perspective, the transmission of Adam's sufferings to his descendants is to be regarded as a fact of nature, one which proceeds only secondarily from his personal will. In the eyes of the Fathers, two other considerations attenuate Adam's responsibility: first, the state of immaturity and inexperience in which Adam was created (cf. St Gregory Palamas, *Theological and Ethical Chapters* 55); and second, the role played by the Devil: on the one hand in goading Adam to sin (cf. St Athanasius, *On the Incarnation of the Word* V.2; St Maximus, *To Thalassios* 61, PG 90.633B)—the author of the Wisdom of Solomon will go so far as to declare that death entered the world because of "the jealousy of the devil" (Wis 2:24); and on the other hand, to spread the effects of evil throughout this world of which he is the "Prince."

[123]The divergence between Eastern and Western thought noted above in this regard is due to a difference in interpretation of this Pauline passage. The Greek text *eph' ō pantes hemarton*, which signifies "because [or "due to the fact that"] all sinned" was translated by the Vulgate as *"in quo omnes peccaverunt"* ("in whom [that is, in Adam] all sinned). The former interpretation, which is that of the Greek Fathers, is accepted today by a majority of exegetes. See J. Meyendorff, *op.cit.*, and S. Lyonnet, "Le sens de *eph' ō* en Rom V, 12 et l'exégèse des Pères grecs," pp. 436-456.

measure' (Is 5:14). Thus, because we imitated the sin which occurred with Adam—to the degree that all have sinned—we became the object of the same condemnation."[124] Still more clearly, Theodoret of Cyrus declares: "It is not because of the sin of our Ancestor that every man is subject to the law of death, but because of his own sin."[125] Without denying the original responsibility of Adam and the hereditary character of fallen human nature,[126] Theodoret wants to affirm that all men are sinful and bear co-responsibility in this inheritance that affects them. By sinning in turn, men contribute towards the perpetuation of Adam's sin and its consequences. In fact, by adding their personal sins to his, they develop and multiply those consequences.

Thus every man, even if he is not *a priori* responsible for the evils suffered by the nature he inherited from Adam, nevertheless becomes *a posteriori* responsible by virtue of his personal transgressions; by thus associating himself with Adam, he in some way assumes Adam's own error and makes it his own.[127] From this point of view, there is a certain solidarity in evil between Adam and his descendants, between all human beings. And every person, as a bearer of human nature, becomes partially responsible, in the degree to which he commits sin, of the evils which come not only upon himself but upon others as well.[128] In this same sense we can understand a teaching of Christ related in the Gospel of St Luke (13:1-5). This does not concern

---

[124] *Commentary on Romans*, PG 74.784BC.

[125] *Commentary on Romans*, PG 82.100.

[126] Cf. ibid.

[127] St Gregory Palamas does not hesitate to attribute to Adam's descendants a responsibility even greater than his, due to their greater experience: "Many people doubtless accuse Adam of having transgressed the divine commandment by allowing himself to be so easily persuaded by the Evil One, and, by virtue of this transgression, to have made us all susceptible to death. But to want to taste some deadly herb before having experience of it is not the same thing as to want to eat it after having such experience and knowing it to be deadly. He who, after having had the experience, nevertheless swallows poison and thereby brings upon himself a miserable death, that death is more blameworthy that is the death of him who, before having had such an experience, makes the same gesture and suffers its consequences. This is why each one of us is much more subject than Adam himself to blame and condemnation." *Theological and Ethical Chapters* 55.

[128] Cf. Mark the Hermit, *Controversy with a Lawyer* 18-19; PG 65.1072-1101.

explicitly the question of illness, but it is nevertheless relevant, since it evokes the reality of a collective responsibility in cases of unfortunate events or accidents which, together with illness and other afflictions that men bear, can be classed among the consequences of sin.[129] To several people who recount the murder of the Galileans ordered by Pilate, Jesus replies: "Do you think that these Galileans were worse sinners than all the other Galileans, because they suffered thus? I tell you, No; but unless you repent you will all likewise perish. Or those eighteen upon whom the tower of Siloam fell and killed them, do you think that they were worse offenders than all the others who dwelt in Jerusalem? I tell you, No; but unless you repent you will all likewise perish." In speaking this way, Christ has no intention of threatening his hearers. Rather, He seeks to teach them that misfortunes of this kind are linked not only to the sins of those who are their victims, but to the sins of humanity as a whole. Although those to whom He is speaking are not the direct cause of what has happened, Jesus nonetheless wants them to feel themselves concerned, implicated and personally responsible for what has happened—and could happen again if they all continue to commit sin. This is why He calls them to repentance.

Faithful to these teachings, Orthodox spirituality—particularly monastic spirituality—has included in its tradition of prayer this intuition concerning our collective responsibility in the face of misfortune that strikes our neighbor, of which illness is merely one expression.[130] Dostoievsky has recalled this tradition in a remarkable declaration made by the starets Zossima: "Each of us is responsible before all, for everyone and for everything."[131]

---

[129]St John Chrysostom holds that "sin is the cause of all evils: the cause of distress, of upheavals, of wars, of illnesses, and the cause of all forms of suffering that come our way and refuse to be healed." *Homilies on Penitence* VII. Again he says: "Sin is the source of all the miseries that afflict men" (ibid.).

[130]Cf. Mark the Hermit, *Controversy with a Lawyer* 20.

[131]*The Brothers Karamazov*, quoted from the French, *Les Frères Karamazov* (Paris: Gallimard, 1972), p. 320.

The Healing of Human Nature by the Incarnate Word

Only Christ can deliver mankind from the consequences of Adam's transgression and from sin itself. As a divine Person, He is able to "enhypostasize" the fullness of human nature. Thereby He assumes human nature totally, restores it by the power of His own divine nature, and reunites and conforms it in Himself to divinity. Thereby He becomes the New Adam, but an Adam who is perfectly fulfilled; and thereby He fully accomplishes the divine plan which the first man failed to bring to completion.[132] "Thus as one man's trespass led to condemnation for all men, so one man's act of righteousness leads to acquittal and life for all men. For as by one man's disobedience many were made sinners, so by one man's obedience many will be made righteous" (Rom 5:18-19). Human nature, fallen in Adam, is restored in Christ and recovers all of the privileges it knew in its prelapsarian state. In the words of St Cyril of Alexandria, "As in Adam man's nature fell ill from corruption, [. . .] so in Christ it has recovered health."[133] By His Incarnation, Christ has overthrown the barrier which separated our nature from God and has opened that

---

[132]Thus Christ accomplished in Himself what the Fathers considered to be the ultimate end of the creation of man: man's deification which, as we have noted, was the mission originally assigned to Adam. Yet man's fulfillment of this ultimate end of his nature presupposes that that nature be in a condition capable of attaining it, that is, that it be in the condition of Adam's own nature before the Fall. This is why, if the ultimate purpose of the Incarnation was to accomplish man's deification (as St Maximus in particular stresses: cf. his *Commentary on the Lord's Prayer*, PG 90.873C; *To Thalassios* 54, PG 90.520D; 60,621A-C), this deification presupposes the restoration of human nature, the destruction of the power of sin and of the devil's tyranny, the victory over death, and the potential restitution to humanity of the incorruptibility and immortality which Adam knew in the beginning; such is the first end of the Incarnation. On the distinction made in Orthodox theology between these two complementary poles of the Incarnation—the saving work and the deifying work of the incarnate Word—see V. Lossky, "Redemption and deification," ch. 5 of *In the Image and Likeness of God* (New York: St Vladimir's Seminary Press, 1974), pp. 97-110. On the work of Christ to accomplish the restoration of human nature, which the Fathers often considered to be a healing, see our study, *Thérapeutique des maladies spirituelles* (Paris, 1991), vol. I, part 3, ch. 1, pp. 319-344, "Le Christ médecin."
[133]*Commentary on Romans* 789B.

nature once more to the deifying energies of uncreated grace. By His
redemptive work, He has freed us from the tyranny of the devil and
destroyed the power of sin. By His death, He has triumphed over
death and corruption. By His resurrection, He has granted us new
and eternal life. And it is not only human nature, but also the creation
as a whole which Christ heals and restores, by uniting it in Himself
with God the Father, thereby abolishing the divisions and ending the
disorders that reigned within it because of sin.

"God," St Maximus writes, "became man in order to save man
from destruction. By reuniting in Himself the ruptures in the universal nature . . . He accomplished the great work of God the Father by
recapitulating all things—things in heaven and things on earth—in
Himself, in whom they also were created. . . . First of all He united us
in Himself, rendering us in total conformity to Himself. Thereby he
restored in us His image, pure and whole, which none of the symptoms of corruption could touch. With us and for us He embraced the
entire creation. . . . He recapitulated all things in Himself, thereby
showing that the entire universe is one, as if it were itself and in its
own manner a human person, fulfilled completely by the reuniting of
its various members. . . . He brought to unity those things that had
been separated; He put an end to the internal war between created
beings, joining together in peace and unbreachable harmony all
things both in heaven and on earth."[134]

Why Does Illness Persist?

This work of Christ, however, does not in any way infringe on human
freedom. His saving work is imposed neither upon mankind nor
upon other created beings. Rather, its accomplishment is offered to
man's free will and presupposes man's acceptance and free collabora-
tion.[135] Replying to those who ask why the grace of salvation was not
imposed on every person, Gregory of Nyssa wrote: "He who holds

---

[134]*Ambigua*, PG 91.1308D-1313B.
[135]Cf. Cyril of Jerusalem, *Baptismal catechism* VII.13.

sovereignty over all things, respecting human freedom to the very
limit, allowed us to have as well our own domain of sovereignty, over
which each of us would be the unique master. This is the domain of
the human will, a faculty which knows no slavery but rather is free,
grounded in the independence of our reason. . . . Our adversaries hold
that God could have led the reluctant by force to accept the Good
News. But where then would be our free will? Where would be
virtue, and the glory of righteous conduct?"[136]

The restoration and deification of human nature accomplished in
the hypostasis of Christ remains potential for human hypostases
unless and until they are incorporated and united in Him. This
incorporation and uniting are accomplished within the Church—
which is the Body of Christ—by the grace of the Holy Spirit communicated in the sacraments. It is necessary, nevertheless, that man
collaborate in this transformation of himself by grace. He must work
(cf. Phil 2:12) to appropriate it; he must open himself to it and assimilate himself to it by constant effort. Through baptism he puts off the
"old man" (Eph 4:22) and puts on Christ (Gal 3:27). Thereby he
becomes the "new man"—but only potentially. He needs to actualize
this transformation in himself from his fallen nature to a restored and
deified nature.[137] This can only occur by virtue of a process of growth
which presupposes first a constant renunciation of the fallen state of
human nature, an ongoing struggle against temptations and self-
purification, and second, acquisition of a renewed nature in Christ by
practicing the commandments. Through this long and difficult
process (cf. Mat 7:14; 11:12), one falls again and again, and no one can
claim to be without sin (cf. 1 Jn 1:8-10; Rom 3:10-12).

Besides, many people simply refuse, through a deliberate exercise
of will, to accept the salvation offered by Christ, and persevere con-
sciously in their choice of evil.

Because sin perpetuates itself in the world, its consequences continue to affect human nature and the cosmos as a whole.

---

[136] *Catechetical Discourse* XXX-XXXI.

[137] See our article, "Le baptême selon saint Maxime le Confesseur," *Revue des sciences religieuses* 65 (1991), 51-70.

It is true that Christ has eliminated the necessity of sin, has put an end to the devil's tyranny, and has removed the sting from death. But He has not ended sin, nor the actions of demons, nor physical death, nor in general the consequences of sin, for He did not want to violate the freedom of the human will which is the cause of these things.[138]

It is only at the end of time and according to the Father's will (cf. Acts 1:7; Mt 24:36) that the restoration of all things will take place and there will appear "a new heaven and a new earth, in which righteousness dwells" (2 Pet 3:13). Then the order and harmony destroyed by sin will be restored and the benefits acquired by Christ in his work of redeeming and deifying our human nature will be fully communicated to all.

The person who dwells in Christ within the Church, where the fullness of grace is to be found, receives the "first-fruits of the Spirit," and tastes of the blessings to come. Sin, the devil, death and corruption no longer hold power over that person and can no longer affect him in any definitive way. The person has been spiritually freed from them.

Nevertheless, the incorruptibility and immortality of which he is assured, and which in a certain way he has already attained, only become reality to his bodily existence after the Resurrection and Last Judgment, just as the deification of his whole being will only be fully accomplished at that ultimate moment (cf. 1 Cor 15:28).

Just as all human beings, by virtue of their common nature, are to a certain extent mutually affected by their sinfulness, and thereby share together in the evil consequences of their sins, so they share together as well in the blessings promised to them. God envisions the salvation and deification not only of every person, but of the entire human race; and in the thought of the Church Fathers, the former is in no way dissociated from the latter. In the words of Origen, "There is only one Body that awaits its redemption."[139] And St Hippolytus

---

[138]Cf. St John of Damascus, *The Orthodox Faith* IV.19; St Irenaeus, *Against Heresies* IV.37.

[139]*Homilies on Leviticus* VII.

writes," God, desiring the salvation of all mankind, calls us to constitute a single 'perfect man.' "[140]

This is why the blessings stored up for us are not granted to us
individually and immediately in their fullness. Rather, there is a delay
in their bestowal as humanity awaits its growth to full stature, according to the possibility offered to each human hypostasis to be saved and
deified. Asked about "the reason why this present painful existence is
not immediately transformed into the existence we long for, but continues in a state of fleshly suffering until the appointed time of the
universal fulfillment when humanity will be delivered from the burden which it bears and will come at last to that state of absolute freedom that characterizes the blessed and imperishable life [to come],"
St Gregory of Nyssa offers the following explanation.[141] When God
created man in the beginning, He did not create an individual but
rather "the fullness [plērōma] of our nature"; "by the divine foreknowledge and power, all of humanity is included in this act." God
knew not only that Adam would sin and, as a consequence would pro-
create, but He knew as well, "He who holds in His hands the limits of
all things," "the exact number of all the individuals who would make
up humanity as a whole." "Whereas the fullness of humanity had been
foreordained by God's foreknowledge, this same God—whose gov-
erning authority orders and delimits all things exactly, and who sees
the future as the present—established in advance the time needed for
the full constitution of the human race, such that the coming of souls
in their predetermined number should determine the limit of time,
and that the flow of time should cease once it were no longer needed
to allow for the propagation of the human race." Accordingly, the end
of time will come "with the fulfillment of human generation;"
"humanity will be transformed and, from its perishable, earthly state,
will become imperishable and eternal" once "the fullness of humanity
shall arrive at its term according to divine foreknowledge, since the
number of souls will no longer have to increase."

---

[140] On the Antichrist.
[141] This is found in chapter XXII of On the Creation of Man (PG 44.204C-205D),
some of the argument having been already developed in ch. XVI, PG 44.185BC.

This solidarity among all people as a consequence of the delay in receiving the fullness of blessings is underscored by the Psalmist: "The righteous will surround me, for Thou wilt deal bountifully with me" (Ps 141/142:8). Still more emphatic is the apostle Paul in his commemoration of the holy patriarchs: "And all these, though well attested by their faith, did not receive what was promised, since God had foreseen something better for us, and that apart from us they should not be made perfect" (Heb 11:39-40). This is St Gregory of Nyssa's understanding of this last passage.[142] But St John Chrysostom also reads it in this way: "Imagine this striking situation of Abraham and of Paul as they await the fulfillment of your happiness before they should receive their full reward. For the Savior told them that they would not receive that reward until we were there to receive it with them. . . . God determined a time when all of us would be crowned together. . . . Abraham and Paul await us as brothers. If all of us constitute one single Body, there is more joy for this Body to be crowned all together than separately, by its individual members."[143]

Although he is a member of the Church where the Kingdom is already present, man in his present bodily condition remains subject to the conditions of this world and to the consequences of sin which hold the cosmos in a state of disorder. For this reason, he is inevitably affected by sickness, suffering and biological death, even if these realities, by the grace of God, receive a new meaning in the context of the spiritual life. Therefore St Maximus can declare: "He who participates in the Spirit is not exempt from the necessities of the body and of human nature."[144] For his part, St Cyprian explains this point by underscoring the solidarity that on the physical plane exists among all men in their earthly state: "For as long as we live in this world, we are linked to the human species by the identity of our body; it is only by the spirit that we are differentiated from it. This is why we share with all men the inconveniences of the flesh, until 'this perishable nature puts on the imperishable' (1 Cor 15:53). When a city is invaded by the

---

[142]Ibid., XXII.208B-D.
[143]*Homilies on Hebrews* XXVIII.1.
[144]*Centuries on Love* III.60.

enemy, its captivity marks all of its inhabitants, without any distinction. And when the clear sky dashes all hope of rain, the drought
threatens everyone equally. Finally, when a ship is hemmed in all
about by rocks, the ensuing shipwreck becomes the common fate of
all the passengers, without exception. So it is with our suffering,
whether it affects our eyes, our limbs or our body as a whole: it affects
us all together, for as long as we all share the same nature in this
world."[145]

In fact it is only in the life beyond, after the body has been resurrected and endowed with incorruptibility, that by the grace of God it
will be totally united and submitted to the soul and entirely spiritu-
alized (cf. 1 Cor 15:44). Although in this present life the body is closely
linked to the soul and can already, together with the soul, be to a certain degree transfigured by the divine energies,[146] in its present reality as a "physical body" (1 Cor 15:44), it possesses its own nature and
destiny.[147] By virtue of its composition and its present mode of existence, the body remains linked to the cosmos and endures the conditions of the fallen created order. Because of its material nature, it is
subject to the laws of matter. As a living organism, it shares the conditions of existence proper to animated beings.[148] And therefore it is
"susceptible of division, of exhaustion, of change" and of alteration.[149]
We can even say that it is "changeable by its nature and unstable by
its essence."[150] Consequently, in our present condition "it is not
possible to escape from illness and to avoid being consumed by age,
for to remain in the same state" is not a property that is ours.[151] In
fact there is an entire portion of the human body that is beyond control of the will, which the person can neither master nor control.[152]

---

[145] On Death 8.

[146] See, for example, St Maximus, Ambigua, PG 91.1088C.

[147] Cf. St John of Damascus, The Orthodox Faith II.12; St Symeon the New Theologian, Catechesis XXV.53-68 and 124-146.

[148] Cf. St John of Damascus, ibid.; St Nicetas Stethatos, On the Soul 32; St John
Chrysostom, Homilies on the Statutes XVIII.3.

[149] St John of Damascus, ibid.

[150] St Symeon the New Theologian, Catechesis XXV.63-66.

[151] Theodorus Petranus, Life of St Theodosius XLVIII.25-49,1-2.

[152] Cf. St John of Damascus, ibid.; St Nicetas Stethatos, On the Soul 31.

St Symeon notes accordingly: "There are many changes in the body, most of which result from human nature (*physis*)."[153]

Therefore the saints themselves inevitably experience both bodily suffering and illness,[154] and in the end biological death. This demonstrates once again that there is no necessary *relationship* between the health of the body and the health of the soul, and that physical sufferings are not directly attributable to the personal sin of those who are afflicted with them. They strike indifferently both the righteous and sinners: "since one fate comes to all, to the righteous and the wicked, to the good and the evil, to the clean and the unclean, to him who sacrifices and him who does not sacrifice. As is the good man, so is the sinner; and he who swears is as he who shuns an oath" (Eccl 9:2; cf. Mt 5:45).

At times, saints are even more afflicted than others. This can be explained for two basic reasons. The first flows from the nature of the divine economy. We shall see in the next chapter that God, without ever being the cause of sickness and suffering, can nevertheless allow them to occur,[155] and he can use them to further the ill person's spiritual progress as well as to serve the spiritual edification of friends and family members. Raising the question, "Why God allows the saints to bear so many afflictions," St John Chrysostom offers eight different but closely related answers. First, to prevent their sublime virtues and their extraordinary works from inspiring pride (cf. 2 Cor 12:7). Second, to prevent others from honoring the saints more than they honor other people, regarding them as gods rather than as simple mortals.[156] In the third place, so that the power of the Lord might make a still greater impact, since it is especially in weakness that his power becomes manifest (cf. 2 Cor 12:9).[157] Fourth, so that the

---

[153] *Catechesis* 53-55; Nicetas Stethatos, ibid.; St John Chrysostom, ibid., XVIII.3.

[154] Cf. St Symeon the New Theologian, *Catechesis* ibid., 122-124; St Gregory of Nazianzen, *Theological Discourse* XVIII.28; St Maximus, *Disputatio cum Bizya II*, PG 90.136-172.

[155] The Fathers consistently respect this nuance and usually use the verb *synkhōrein*, which means "concede," "consent to," "accept," "authorize" or "permit." Or again they use the verb *parakhōrein* which has a similar span of meanings.

[156] See St Barsanuphius, *Letters* 559.

[157] Cf. *The Life of St Theodore of Sykeon* 105.

patience of the saints itself might make a greater impression, demonstrating to others that they serve God disinterestedly, with a pure
love, since in the midst of their tribulations they remain equally
devoted to him. In the fifth place, their suffering leads us to meditate
on the resurrection of the dead; for when one sees a just and virtuous
man leave this life only after having suffered an infinite number of
ills, one can only focus on future judgment which will demonstrate in
one's regard the righteousness of God. Sixth, it is so that those who
experience adversities might be relieved and consoled by seeing that
the holiest of people have experienced the same things and even
worse. Seventh, it is so that the sublime character of their actions will
not lead the rest of us to think that they were of another nature than
ours and that we can in no way imitate them (cf. Jas 5:17; Wis 7:1).
And eighth, it is to teach us what constitutes true happiness and
unhappiness: true happiness is to be united with God by a virtuous
life, whereas the only true cause of misery is to be separated from
God.[158]

Another fundamental reason why the saints are often afflicted
even more than other people with illness concerns the direct action
of demons, which attempt through various afflictions to trouble
them, to disturb their inner activity, and to turn them away from their
essential work. Evagrius several times stresses that when the spirit of
a man is united to God in prayer, the devil—having no direct control
over his soul and nevertheless trying to create trouble for him—has
no other recourse than to act upon the body.[159] Then the devil does
violence to him, even to the point of modifying his constitution (*kra-
sis*). Because of the link between body and soul, he hopes that by
altering the bodily state he will bring disturbance to the soul, leading
it to accept thoughts and fantasies[160] that are foreign to prayer, and to
excite passions within it.[161] St John Chrysostom adds, "Just a minor

---

[158]*Homilies on the Statutes* I.6-8. Cf. St Gregory of Nazianzus, *Theological Discourse* XVIII.28.

[159]*On Prayer* 63 and 68. See the commentary of I. Hausherr, pp. 90f and 99f in
his edition of this treatise (Paris, 1960), and the further references given there.

[160]Ibid., 63.

[161]Ibid., 68.

change in the constitution of the body can trouble the soul in a great many of its functions."[162] In addition to these disturbances—often rather benign, but which can reach the point where they create real illnesses—the demons can introduce into the bodies of the saints, in various forms and under various circumstances, disorders of much greater importance, causing them to endure terrible suffering. The Desert Mother Syncletica remarks: "Overcome by health, the devil makes the body ill."[163] In fact, he cannot bear that a man should devote all the energy of his being to worshiping God. By means of these afflictions and by reducing the physical powers of the saints, the devil weakens the power of their spirit and reduces the intensity of their worship. Depriving them of the resources of bodily health, he attempts to limit their vigilance, to distract their attention, to decrease their resistance to temptation, to ruin their ascetic effort, and finally to drive them to despair of divine assistance and—if indeed possible—to curse God.

The case of Job offers us a particularly clear example of these diabolical intentions aimed against the righteous. The prologue to the Book of Job reveals clearly not only the direct action of the devil in producing illness (2:6-7), but his purpose in so doing (2:5). But, as the Book of Job also makes clear, sickness and suffering, although not caused by God, can become part of his divine Providence. Leaving intact the free will of the devil or of the person who commits some evil act, God can modify its effects by granting to the afflicted person the power to use the suffering he experiences for his own spiritual good. Imposing certain limits on the diabolical activity (cf. Job 1:12; 2:6) and preventing the afflicted person from being tempted beyond his capacity to withstand (1 Cor 10:13), God allows the devil to inflict such evils upon the righteous, since he knows that those who manage to bear them while remaining faithful to him will reap huge spiritual benefits which otherwise, following their own way, they could never come to know.

---

[162]*Homilies on the Statutes* II.4. Cf. St Maximus, *Centuries on Love* II.92; St Symeon the New Theologian, loc. cit., 184-190.

[163]*Apophthegmata* (alphabetical series), *Syncletica* 7 (see B. Ward, *The Sayings of the Desert Fathers*, London: Mowbrays,1975, p. 194).

ILLNESSES OF THE BODY AND ILLNESSES OF THE SOUL

In these latter instances, the causal relation "personal sin—sickness" is seen to be not only denied but actually reversed. The illnesses of the body, far from being directly engendered by illnesses of the soul, are to the contrary provoked by the *health* of the soul. The absence of any such causal relation is further confirmed by the fact that we find, next to saints who suffer grave illnesses, multitudes of sinners whose bodies are flourishing with health (and in many passages of Scripture we find a reaction of surprise to this double paradox: see, for example, Jer 12:1; 5:8; Job ch. 21; Ps 72/73:4-5; Mal 3:15).

The Fathers admit, nonetheless, that in certain cases illnesses can very well be linked to the sinful state of those they afflict.[164] Accordingly, although he considers that in principle "illness does not depend on us," St Maximus affirms that a disordered life could very well be its cause.[165] In a similar vein, St Barsanuphius speaks of "illnesses that come from negligence and disorder."[166] And St Nicholas Cabasilas states in a still more categorical way: "There are those persons who are afflicted by bodily illnesses caused by the moral depravation of the soul."[167]

To the degree that "the passions leave their imprint on the body," as St Gregory of Nazianzus puts it,[168] it becomes undeniable, in the words of St Seraphim of Sarov, that "illness may very well be engendered by the passions."[169] St Nicholas Stethatos, for his part, generally incriminates *philautia* or egotistical self-love—considered by Eastern ascetic tradition as the primordial passion—as the passion which engenders all others and contains all others within itself.[170] The chief cause of illness, however, are those passions which the

---

[164]Cf. St Seraphim of Sarov's (unspecified) quotation of St Basil: "Remove sin and illnesses disappear." Quoted in I. Goraïnoff, *Séraphim de Sarov* (Paris, 1979), p. 208.

[165]*Dispute with Bizya* II.

[166]*Letters*, 521.

[167]*Commentary on the Divine Liturgy* XLIII.2.

[168]*Theological Discourses* XXXII.27. He gives numerous examples.

[169]Loc. cit.

[170]See I. Hausherr, *Philautie*, Rome, 1952.

ascetic tradition calls "bodily," not because they have their source in the body itself, but because they can only manifest themselves through the body, finding their basis in the body's tendencies, such as *gastrimargia* or gluttony,[171] together with *porneia*, which in the ascetic literature signifies sexual passions in general.[172] To these we can add *akēdia*, the weariness of soul which engenders listlessness of the body;[173] irascibility, which produces well-known physiological disturbances;[174] as well as fear[175] and sadness.[176]

Aside from illnesses related to passions such as these, we can find in the Scriptures a few cases of afflictions that undoubtedly arise as direct consequences of personal sins (cf. Num 12:10; 2 Kg 5:27; 2 Chr 21:18; 26:19; 1 Sam 3:17-18). It is appropriate to give a positive reading to these cases, that by the way are rare. We should not read into them some naive notion of punishment, whether out of anger or as a mechanical reflex, inflicted by divine wrath. Rather, they represent providential ways to salvation, in that for the persons concerned they serve most adequately to lead them to recognize, through the sudden misery of their body, both the illness of their soul and their estrangement from God. In addition, such cases also represent a reminder to others—with the aim of calling them to repentance—of the fundamental, ontological link that unites illness, suffering and death to the sin of everyone.

---

[171]See, for example, Sir 37:29-31. St John Chrysostom, *Homilies on John* XXXVIII.1; *Treatise on virginity* 69; St Basil, *Longer Rule*, 19; St Maximus, *Centuries on Love* II.74; St Nicholas Stethatos, *Centuries* I.88; St Symeon the New Theologian, *Catechism* XX.132-133.

[172]See, for example, St John Chrysostom, *Homilies on Philippians* XIV.2; St Maximus, *Commentary on the Lord's Prayer* (PG 90,889B).

[173]See, for example, St John Chrysostom, Homilies on John XXXVIII.1. The term *akēdia* embraces a multitude of nuances, including disgust, boredom, weariness, exhaustion, discouragement, dissatisfaction, and apathy or torpor.

[174]See, for example, St John Chrysostom, *Homilies on Acts* VI.3; *Homilies on John* XXVI.3; St Gregory of Nazianzus, PG 37,816A and 948A; *Discourse* XXXII.27; St John Climacus, *Ladder* VIII.5; St John of Damascus, *The Orthodox Faith* II.16.

[175]Cf. St Gregory of Nazianzus, *Discourse* XXXII.27.

[176]Cf. St Gregory of Nazianzus, ibid. The nature and pathological effects of these various passions are analyzed at length in our study, *Thérapeutique des maladies spirituelles*, I (Paris, 1991), p. 151-306.

Besides these cases, which are striking for their particularity, we cannot deny the general influence that the state of the soul exercises over the state of the body, due on the one hand to their close relation to the very nature of human life, and on the other to the spiritual link we have just noted. This influence promotes illness in those who remain in submission to sin and the passions. Spiritual disorders inevitably express themselves in soul and body by ailments that are often imperceptible to the untrained observer. The saints, however, know how to read their presence on a person's face, or else they sense their manifestation in certain circumstances, thanks to the gift of discernment which they possess. Conversely, in the experience of those who purify their passions by divine-human asceticism, the influence of the soul on the body becomes a source of purification. When the soul participates in divine peace and in the power of divine grace, it communicates this peace and this grace to the functions of the body.[177] This is why a great many holy people attain a ripe old age and preserve even at the bodily level a remarkable vigor and surprising youthfulness.[178] Whereas certain saints have as their calling to suffer in their body trials of suffering and corruption, it is granted to others to manifest the holiness which, by divine grace, they have achieved within their soul. Their body, also penetrated by the divine energies, reveals its destiny as one that transcends the ordinary fate of matter. St John Climacus writes in this regard: "When a man is united and filled within with divine love, we can behold in his body, as though reflected by a mirror, the brightness and serenity of his soul, just as it happened to Moses when, after he had been honored with the vision

---

[177]The soul which lives in divine peace and in hope of the blessings of the Kingdom finds itself, for example, liberated from all emotional disturbance and anxiety and consequently from their pathological influence on the body. The pacifying role of hesychast prayer on cardiac and respiratory rhythms is well known, as are their beneficial effects on the entire organism. St Maximus states in a general manner: "A well-ordered life is itself the cause of health" (*Dispute with Bizya* II).

[178]This point has often been noted in the *Lives* of the saints. See, for example, Calinicos, *Life of Hypatios* 26.4. Evagrius notes in this regard: "We who dwell in the desert are rarely ill" (*On the diverse evil thoughts* XI; PG 79.1200-1233; PG 40.1240-1244).

of God, his face shone with light."[179] And he adds: "I believe that the bodies of those persons who have become incorruptible are not as susceptible to illness as others are, for, having been purified by the all pure flame of divine love, they are no longer subject to any form of corruption."[180] As the first to experience in this world the foretaste of the Transfiguration and Resurrection granted by Christ to the entire human race, these holy people bear witness to all mankind of the end of all illness through the total healing of human nature accomplished by the "supreme Physician of soul and body." And by that witness they offer to the world that same foretaste as a promise of the greater and more complete state of health that shall be known in the Kingdom of God.

THE PRECARIOUSNESS OF HEALTH

Nevertheless, for them as for all mankind, perfect health of the body during this life can never be attained. In this world perfect health never exists in absolute form; health is always a matter of partial and temporary equilibrium.[181] We can even say that health in this present age is simply a matter of a lesser illness. The very notion of ideal health is, in fact, beyond our comprehension,[182] since it reflects no experience known to us in this life. In our present condition, "health" is always in some sense "illness" that has simply not appeared as such and/or is not significant enough to be identified as such.[183]

---

[179] *The Ladder of Divine Ascent* XXX.17.

[180] Ibid. XXX.19.

[181] Cf. St Symeon the New Theologian, *Catechesis* XXV.124-126.

[182] This is what has provoked endless philosophical and medical debates which aim to define the meaning and scope of the concept "health."

[183] This is what allows medicine to extend and to refine more and more its definition of illness. It also leads to the increasing "medicalization" of the individual in modern society, by which medical experts attempt at all costs to identify as illnesses states that in earlier ages were never considered to be such.

2.

The Spiritual Meaning of Illness

THE AMBIVALENCE OF HEALTH AND ILLNESS

"Among human affairs," St John Cassian writes, "nothing merits being held as good in the true sense of the word except virtue, which leads us to God and makes us adhere to this immutable Good. On the other hand, there is no evil other than sin, which, by separating us from God who is good, unites us to the devil who is evil."[1]

It is true that physical health corresponds to the normal state of human nature—that is, its prelapsarian state—and for that reason health can be considered as good in itself.[2] Nevertheless, from another point of view health is worthless to the human person—it does not constitute a true good but is only good in appearance[3]—if it is not used well,[4] that is, if it is not used with an aim toward the Good: to fulfill the commandments of Christ and to glorify God. This is why St Basil declares: "Insofar as it does not render good those who possess it, health cannot be counted among those things that are good by nature."[5] In fact it is evil if it contributes to making a person indifferent to his salvation, keeps him away from God by giving him the false impression that he is self-sufficient, and bestows on him that strength of the flesh which actually weakens, rather than giving him that weakness in which God reveals himself, which constitutes true

---

[1]*Conferences* VI.3. Cf. St John Chrysostom, *Homilies on the Statutes* V.2; St Basil, *Homily: God is not the cause of sufferings* 5.

[2]Cf. St Maximus the Confessor, *Centuries on Love* II.77.

[3]Ibid.

[4]Ibid.

[5]*Letters* CCXXXVI.7.

strength (2 Cor 12:9-10). Health is an even greater evil if it is used to give free rein to the passions, thereby becoming an instrument of iniquity (Rom 6:13). "Know, then," St Gregory of Nazianzus counsels us, "how to despise an insidious health that leads to sin."[6]

As for illness, it is in itself something evil to the extent that it arises as a consequence of the sin of Adam and as an effect of demonic activity within the fallen world. As such, it is a negation of the order God intended when he created the world and mankind. Nonetheless, it is evil only on the level of physical nature and the body. If one does not give oneself over to it entirely, illness cannot injure one's soul, nor can it affect one's essential being, one's spiritual nature. According to Christ's own teaching, a person should fear whatever can make perish in Gehenna both body and soul, but he need have no fear of what can affect his body alone, without bringing death to his soul (Mt 10:28). By itself illness does not have the power to separate man from God; therefore from a spiritual point of view it cannot be considered to be a source of evil in his life. St John Chrysostom notes: "If the soul is in good health, bodily illness can in no way harm a man."[7] Illness, then, is only evil in appearance.[8] It can even constitute a blessing for man[9] in the sense that, if one uses it appropriately,[10] one can draw from it considerable spiritual benefit, thereby making of what was originally a sign of mortality into an instrument of salvation.[11] St John Chrysostom adds: "There is evil which, properly speaking, is not evil, even though it bears that name: such as illness, and other things of that sort. If they were truly evil, they would not be able to become for us the source of a multitude of blessings."[12] In the same vein St John Cassian states: "How can we see [in illness] something that is essentially evil, since it serves as a

---

[6]*Discourse* XIV.34.

[7]*Homilies on Lazarus* VI.5.

[8]St John Chrysostom, *Homilies on the demons* I.5; St John of Damascus, *The Orthodox Faith* IV.19; St Basil, *Homily: God is not the cause of sufferings* 5.

[9]Cf. St Barsanuphius, *Letters* 78; St John Chrysostom, *Homilies on Annas* I.2.

[10]St Peter of Damascus, *Book* I.

[11]St John Chrysostom, *Homilies on Penitance* VII.6.

[12]*Homilies on the demons* I.5.

blessing to so many by granting them the means to attain to abundant and eternal joy?"[13]

Finally, St Gregory of Nazianzus offers the following counsel: "Do not admire every form of health, and do not condemn every illness."[14]

Consequently, in certain cases and from the point of view of that which is spiritually good for man, illness can be paradoxically considered as a higher good than health and therefore as preferable to health.[15] St Gregory of Nazianzus observes that the aim of medical treatment "consists in reconfirming health or the good condition of the flesh if such exists, or in recovering it if it has been lost. But it is not clear that these advantages are really useful. Often, in fact, the opposite conditions are more advantageous to those who are affected by them."[16] Accordingly, we encounter any number of holy people, faced with their own illnesses or the illnesses of those in their care, who ask God not in the first place for a return to health, but for what is spiritually the most useful. And rather than lament because of these illnesses, they rejoice in the benefits that can be drawn from them.[17]

THE POSITIVE MEANING OF SICKNESS AND SUFFERING

Such an attitude, however, presupposes that we attribute to illness a meaning and a finality that transcend physical nature.

To consider illness strictly as a phenomenon unto itself is almost inevitably to see it in a negative, sterile light; and this only increases the physical suffering and moral pain which result from a sense of its absurdity. The consequence of such an attitude is generally to leave the way open to the activity of demons and to develop in the soul troubling passions, such as fear, anxiety, anger, weariness, revolt and despair. These states not only do not relieve the body, they most often

---

[13] *Conferences* VI.6.
[14] Loc. cit.
[15] Cf., for example, St Barsanuphius, *Letters* 189, 513, 570.
[16] *Discourse* II.22.
[17] Cf. St Barsanuphius, *Letters* 90, 220, 570; St John of Gaza, *Letters* 148, 384.

increase the symptoms of the evil that affects it, thereby creating sickness even in the soul.[18] The illness then serves no good at all, but it becomes for the ill person a source of spiritual deterioration which puts his soul in jeopardy perhaps more than it does his body.

It is because of this very danger that the Fathers stress the point that "it is not in vain, nor without reason, that we are subject to illnesses."[19] This is why they encourage us to be vigilant when illness strikes,[20] and not to trouble ourselves first of all with their natural causes and means to cure them. Rather, our first concern should be to discern their meaning within the framework of our relationship to God, and to throw light on the positive function they can have in furthering our salvation. In this respect St Maximus counsels: "When you are exposed to unexpected testing . . . search out its purpose and you will find the means to profit from it."[21] The ideal, then, is to avoid from the beginning allowing ourselves to be dominated by suffering when it exists, but to go beyond the limits in which the suffering tends to enclose the soul and even our entire being, our entire existence. In this double perspective St Gregory of Nazianzus offers the following counsel to an ill acquaintance: "I don't wish and I don't consider it good that you, well instructed in divine things as you are, should suffer the same feelings as more worldly people, that you should allow your body to give in, that you should agonize over your suffering as if it were incurable and irredeemable. Rather, I should want you to be philosophical about your suffering and show yourself superior to the cause of your affliction, beholding in the illness a superior way towards what is ultimately good for you."[22]

To be philosophical about one's illness and suffering means above all for a person to consider what they reveal to him about his condition.

As a consequence of Adamic sin and an effect of sin perpetuated in the fallen world, together with demonic activity, illness manifests

---

[18]St John Chrysostom, *Homilies on the Statutes* V.4.
[19]Ibid. *Homilies on Annas* I.2.
[20]Ibid. *Homilies on the Statutes* V.4.
[21]*Centuries on Love* II.42.
[22]*Letters* XXXI.2-3.

the misery of a humanity separated from God.[23] In the corruption and suffering of the body, one experiences the weakness of one's earthly being, the ephemeral character of one's existence in this world, and, generally speaking, one's fragility, inadequacy, contingency and personal limits.[24] The illness of the body reminds us of the illness of our entire fallen nature. The loss of health appears as the symbol and perceptible sign of the loss of paradisiacal life. By confining the soul within the limits of the body, sickness and suffering destroy any illusions of fullness and self-sufficiency a person may previously have had, illusions fueled by a state of health he took for granted. They teach a person the extent of their poverty, even their ontological nakedness (Gen 3:7), and remind him that he is dust (3:19). The person can no longer consider himself as absolute, since his fundamental pride is broken. St John Climacus comments on this positive function of illness: "Sometimes the purpose of illness is to humiliate our spirit."[25] Similarly, St John Chrysostom: "It is for our good that we are victims of illnesses . . . , since the pride stirred up within us by relaxed attention finds a cure in this weakness and in these afflictions."[26] And he adds that it is because the safeguard of illness was lacking in the beginning "that the first man allowed himself to be carried away by pride."[27] St Seraphim says more tersely that by virtue of illness "man comes back to himself."[28]

Because it undermines us at the level of our being, illness often challenges our former, false equilibrium, and leads us to question the very foundations of our existence. It effectively weakens our impassioned attachments to this world.[29] And in so doing, it reveals the vanity of those attachments and leads us to surpass their limits.

---

[23]See the section on original sin in ch. 1 above.

[24]Cf. St John Chrysostom, *Homilies on 2 Timothy* X.

[25]*The Ladder of Divine Ascent* XXVI.37; Cf. St Isaac the Syrian, *Ascetic Discourse* 21; St Nicetas Stethatos, *Centuries* I.87.

[26]*Homilies on Annas* I.2.

[27]Ibid.

[28]*Spiritual Instructions*, in I. Goraïnov, *Séraphim de Sarov* (Paris, 1979), p. 208.

[29]Ibid.

"Sickness," St Nicetas Stethatos remarks, "diminish the earthly sentiments of the soul."[30]

One's spiritual intelligence—purified of these burdens that alienate it from the flesh, and refined by suffering[31]—perceives another, spiritual world; and the purified will aspires to it, and elevates the soul to participate in it. Thus Dostoïevsky can write: "A healthy man is always an earthly, material man . . . But as soon as he falls ill, and the normal, earthly order of his organism is disturbed, then the possibility of another world makes itself known to him at once; and as the illness worsens, his relations with this world become ever closer."[32]

Understood and experienced in this perspective, illness does not crush a person under the weight of their "mortal body" (Rom 7:24), but to the contrary turns the person toward God. It reunites the person to God, drawing him toward God as the true source and end of his existence. It offers wisdom to his intelligence—that is, true knowledge of the world, of himself and of God—and to his will it offers conformity to the will of his Creator. "God does not permit illness to debase us," St John Chrysostom declares, "but because he wanted to make us better, more wise, and more submissive to his will, which is the basis of our salvation."[33]

A Manifestation of Providence

From what we have said, it is clear that divine Providence is at work in our illness. To "be philosophical" about that illness means to strive to discover the intentions and aims of God with regard to ourselves.

In every illness, God speaks to us about our salvation and expresses his will to help us in attaining it.

---

[30]*Centuries* I.87.

[31]Dostoïevsky often underscored this capacity of suffering to awaken and develop the conscience. In *A Writer's Journal* (from the French, *Le Journal d'un écrivain*, Paris: Gallimard, 1951, p. 371) he can even draw the conclusion: "A man with a conscience is by that very fact a man who suffers."

[32]*Crime and Punishment* (from the French, *Crime et châtiment*, Paris: Gallimard, 1950, p. 342).

[33]*Homilies on Annas* I.2.

Illness, the Fathers often stress, manifests a divine pedagogy.[34] In the same spirit they add that illness represents a correction that God inflicts on man because of his sins.[35] This correction should not be understood in a negative sense as punishment or chastisement, but rather in a positive sense expressed by the Latin verb *corrigere*, which signifies to correct, reform, ameliorate or heal.[36] In this perspective, it seems that God wills, or at least authorizes and, in any case, makes use of illness for man's well-being,[37] to correct within him those things which sin has distorted or perverted, and to heal him of his spiritual ills.[38] Thus, paradoxically, the illness of the body becomes, by divine Providence, a remedy which promotes healing of the soul. St Isaac the Syrian, addressing a man "afflicted by the illnesses and agonies of the body," writes: "Be vigilant over yourself and consider the multitude of remedies that the true Physician sends to you for the health of your inner man."[39] And he adds: "God brings illnesses for the health of the soul."[40]

The unpleasantness, the pain and the suffering that accompany illnesses, therefore, should be considered in the same way as the usually inevitable side-effects of medicines used by physicians. As St John Chrysostom remarks, if we accept the latter, all the more we should accept those that come from God. For he engages us in a therapy that is much more basic than the one proposed by doctors: "The physician is not only a physician when he orders baths, adequate nourishment, and when he orders the patient to walk through flower

---

[34]Cf., for example, St Barsanuphius, *Letters* 515; St John of Gaza, *Letters* 643.

[35]Cf., for example, St Barsanuphius, *Letters* 78, 513, 515, 516, 521, 613; St John of Gaza, *Letters* 148.

[36]The term the Greek Fathers usually choose is *paideia*, which in a positive sense means "education." It is derived from the verb *paideuein*, which signifies "instruct," "raise" or "train," at the same time that it suggests "correct." *Paideia* must be associated with *paidagōgia*, whose meaning is examined in note 38 below.

[37]Cf. for example, St Barsanuphius, *Letters* 521.

[38]We should note that the term "pedagogy" derives from the Greek word *paidagōgia*, which, in addition to "education," signifies the care one gives to a person who is ill. Clement of Alexandria thus calls Christ *o paidagōgos*, meaning he who educates and directs, but also he who treats the sick.

[39]*Ascetic Discourse* 8.

[40]Ibid., 5.

gardens, but also when he burns and cuts. . . . Thus, knowing that God loves us more than all the physicians combined, we need not worry nor have any need to ask him to justify the means he employs. Rather, whether he wants to be indulgent or severe, let us abandon ourselves to him. For by either of these means, his desire is always to save us and to unite us to himself."[41]

In the same vein, St John Climacus remarks that the pain that accompanies illness is like that we experience in using certain medicines. It is only subjectively an evil; objectively, it serves for the good of the person it affects: "Properly speaking, afflictions are not evils; but they appear to be such in the eyes of those who are struck by them for their own good. . . . In fact, however salutary iron and fire may be for treating a gangrenous wound, and however charitable the hand of the doctor may be who uses them, in the eyes of the patient their use is an evil. Every teaching seems bitter at the time to those it is intended to form, just as the apostle declares: "For the moment all discipline seems painful rather than pleasant; later it yields the peaceful fruit of righteousness to those who have been trained by it" (Heb 12:11).[42]

God knows better than we do what it is that we need.[43] He gives to each one of us what is spiritually most useful.[44] He heals and saves each person by the ways that are best adapted to that person's personality, specific state and particular situation.[45] If, in order to do this, he often uses illness as a means, it is because illness by its very nature is a particularly appropriate instrument for awakening a person's spirit that has fallen into the sluggishness of sin. Thereby God makes the person, by virtue of the evil that afflicts his body, aware of a less apparent evil that afflicts his soul; for without that bodily suffering, the person would remain indifferent to the state of their soul, or in any case would be less sensitive to it.

---

[41] *Homily on the Paralytic* 2.

[42] *Conferences* VI.3.

[43] Cf., for example, St John Chrysostom, *Homily on the Paralytic* 2; St Barsanuphius, *Letters* 90; St John of Gaza, *Letters* 79.

[44] Cf. St John Chrysostom, ibid.; St Barsanuphius, *Letters* 190, 223, 525.

[45] Cf. St Maximus, *Centuries on Love* II.44.

This is the point St John Chrysostom makes, when he says: "Ordinarily we experience no pain when the soul is sick, yet on the contrary when the body is troubled we use every means possible to relieve that trouble. For this very reason God afflicts the body because of the sins of the soul, in order to restore health to man's most noble aspect by making use of the least noble affliction. This is the way St Paul corrects the incestuous Corinthian (1 Cor 5): he mortifies his flesh in order to save his soul. The incision he makes in his body cures his vice."[46] The same saint elsewhere stresses the power that illness possesses on a spiritual level to awaken us from laziness, to stimulate our activity and to awaken our attention.[47]

In a similar vein St Isaac the Syrian teaches that it is "so they do not succumb to the dullness of negligence," and in order to "awaken their spirit" that "He who watches over man" sometimes places ill-nesses of the body before those of the soul, thus helping them by this means to come closer to God.[48] And again he explains that God gives us the opportunity by various ways to "discover our life" and to attain his Kingdom. He who is himself afflicted by a voluntary asceticism, St Isaac says, "the mercy of God follows him and the love of God for mankind comforts him." Yet, he adds, "the souls of those whose will is too weak to allow them to possess their own life . . . God leads to virtue by making them undergo afflictions they do not want. Never-theless, by this second way, man finally attains the same blessings as by the first way. Thus, "the poor Lazarus was not deprived of the goods of this world by a gesture of his free will, rather his body was tormented by wounds; yet in the end he was honored by being taken up into the bosom of Abraham."[49]

---

[46] *Homilies on John* XXXVIII.1; cf. St Maximus, *Centuries on Love* II.44,46.

[47] *Homilies on the Demons* I.5. Cf. *Commentary on Psalm IV* 3. St Nicetas Stethatos similarly remarks that illnesses "make the energy of the soul stronger and more intense" (*Centuries* I.87).

[48] *Ascetic Discourses* 21.

[49] Ibid., 25.

AN OPPORTUNITY FOR SPIRITUAL PROGRESS

There are two ways in which we can say that illness is due to sin. In the first place, illness occurs as a consequence of "original" sin, a factor common to the descendants of Adam, or as the result of some personal sin. In the second place, illness occurs as a means given by God for man's purification from sin. This "cathartic" function of illness is often stressed by the Fathers,[50] who take up St Peter's affirmation, "whoever has suffered in the flesh has ceased from sin" (1 Pet 4:1). St John Chrysostom states: "Afflictions, illnesses, ill health and the pains that our bodies experience . . . are counted for the remission of our trespasses."[51] And he sees these afflictions "the furnace in which we are purified."[52] St Barsanuphius writes to one of his spiritual sons: "All that God allows your body to suffer serves toward lightening the burden of your sins."[53] Amma Syncletica teaches a similar theme: "If illness weighs us down, let us not be sorrowful . . . for all these things are for our good, for the purification of our desires."[54] St Isaac the Syrian notes in a similar sense: "Afflictions kill the pleasure of the passions."[55] For his part, St John Climacus remarks that "illness sometimes has as its aim to purify us from our sins."[56] In a similar vein St John Chrysostom underscores the paradox: "Suffering is imposed on us because of sin, and it is suffering that delivers us from sin. . . . Sin gives birth to suffering, and suffering brings death to sin."[57] And the holy prophet Isaiah celebrates this transformation: "Behold, it was for my salvation that I bore great suffering" (Is 38:17).

---

[50]See St Maximus, *Centuries on Love* I.76; St Gregory of Nazianzus, *Letters* XXXI.3; St Ilias the Presbyter, *Gnomic Anthology* I.9 (P.G. 127.1129-1148; G.E.H. Palmer, P. Sherrard, K. Ware, *The Philokalia*, vol. 3, London: Faber, 1984, p. 35).

[51]*Homily on the parable of the debtor* 5.

[52]*Homily on the paralytic* 2.

[53]*Letters* 72.

[54]B. Ward, *The Sayings of the Desert Fathers. The alphabetical collection*, London/Oxford: Mowbray's 1975, p. 194-195.

[55]*Ascetic Discourse* 27.

[56]*Ladder*, XXVI.37.

[57]*Homilies on repentance* VII.6.

By the grace of Christ the illness of the body can thus serve as a remedy for the ailments of the soul. Thereby what was originally for man an effect of his fall can become an instrument for his salvation. St Maximus the Confessor demonstrates how Christ transformed the meaning of pain by his Passion: whereas before it was the just consequence of sin—and in some sense a debt that our nature had to pay because of sin—Christ, by his unjust suffering, makes of it a means to condemn our sin and to grant us access to divine life.[58] By virtue of his baptism, man becomes by grace a participant in the Passion, Death and Resurrection of Christ. He receives from the Holy Spirit the power to work out a transfiguration of suffering in the context of his personal existence.

Illness and its attendant sufferings often make up part of the numerous tribulations through which a person must pass in order to enter the Kingdom of God (Acts 14:22). They constitute a part of the cross which the person must take up and carry, in order to be worthy of Christ, to follow him on the way of salvation which he has opened for us (cf. Mt 10:38; 16:24; Mk 8:34; Lk 9:23; 14:27), to live and receive fully the grace received from him through baptism, to assimilate oneself truly to him, to suffer and to die with him, in order to rise again and live in eternal communion with him (2 Cor 4:10-12). St Macarius teaches: "He who wants to be an imitator of Christ, so that he too may be called a son of God, born of the Spirit, must above all bear courageously and patiently the afflictions he encounters, whether these be bodily illnesses, slander and vilification from men, or attacks from the unseen spirits."[59] "Without tasting of Christ's sufferings with understanding of their significance, the soul will never be in communion with him," adds St Isaac the Syrian.[60]

Because they contribute to the mortification of the flesh—the destruction of passions which constitute the old Adam[61]—illness and

---

[58] *Questions to Thalassios* 61, PG 90.625D-641B.
[59] St Symeon Metaphrastes, *Paraphrase of the Homilies of St Makarios of Egypt* 129; Palmer, Sherrard, Ware, *The Philokalia* vol. 3 (London: Faber & Faber, 1984), p. 342.
[60] *Ascetic Discourses* 5.
[61] Cf., for example, *Apophthegmata*, alph., *Syncletica* 10; St Maximus, *Questions to Thalassios* 47; PG 90.428a; St Seraphim of Sarov, *Spiritual Instructions*, loc. cit.

the sufferings which accompany it represent various forms of asceticism (fasting, vigils, different forms of physical labor)[62] which aim to eliminate passions. Of these, as St Gregory Palamas notes, pain "kills the sinfulness of the body and moderates those thoughts which provoke brute passions."[63] Consequently, sickness and suffering can take the place of ascetic practices and thereby free those afflicted by them from the need to exercise those practices. Thus St Syncletica can affirm: "Fasting and sleeping on the ground are prescribed for us because of pleasures. But if illness weakens these pleasures, there is no longer any justification for these practices."[64] Conversely, the person who voluntarily assumes the sufferings of traditional asceticism is often spared of those provoked by illness.[65]

At the same time that God uses illness to purify man of his sins and passions, he grants him to rediscover the way of the virtues and to make progress in them.[66] "The more God afflicts us," St John Chrysostom notes, "the more he perfects us."[67] In fact, sickness and its attendant sufferings, with other tribulations, appear to be a condition for acquiring the virtues and the virtuous life in general. St Isaac the Syrian writes in this regard: "If we love virtue, then it is impossible that the body not suffer from illness."[68]

In sickness the Christian finds first of all an opportunity to manifest and to strengthen his faith. St Cyrpian affirms, "What makes us different from those who do not know God is that they grumble and complain about their misfortune, whereas for us tribulation, far from turning us from true courage and authentic faith, fortifies us through

---

[62]*Syncletica* 10; St John Chrysostom, *Homilies on Annas* I.2; St Barsanuphius, *Letters* 348; St John Carpathios, *Century* 68.

[63]Loc. cit.

[64]Loc. cit. Cf. St Barsanuphius, *Letters* 23, 77, 79; St John Carpathios, loc. cit.; St John of Damascus, *On the Virtues and Vices, Philokalia, op. cit.,* vol 2, p. 334-342; St Seraphim of Sarov, *Spiritual Instructions,* loc. cit. This is why St Dorotheus of Gaza lessens the fasting requirements for his spiritual child Dositheus when the latter falls ill (*Life of St Dositheus,* 11).

[65]Cf. St Isaac the Syrian, *Ascetic Discourse* 24 and 34.

[66]Ibid., 25.

[67]*Homilies on Lazarus* VI.8.

[68]*Ascetic Discourses* 4.

suffering. Thus, whether we are exhausted from the tearing of our innards, or a violent interior burning consumes us from the stomach to the throat, or our strength is constantly sapped because of vomiting, or our eyes are shot through with blood, or we are eaten by gangrene and forced to amputate a member of our body, or some infirmity suddenly deprives us of the use of our legs, our sight or our hearing: all of these afflictions are just so many opportunities to deepen our faith."[69]

In the second place, illness offers us the opportunity to acquire the fundamental virtue of patience,[70] and to attain even to its highest degree. For, as St John Chrysostom expresses it, "if patience in general is preeminent with respect to the other virtues, patience in suffering is preeminent with respect to all other forms of patience."[71] And he explains this further: as "illness is the most unbearable of all evils, it is by bearing illness that one demonstrates above all the virtue of patience."[72]

Patience acquired in this manner becomes the source of numerous spiritual benefits.[73] It is in fact the source of many other virtues: first of all, hope, as St Paul declares: "suffering produces patience [*hypomonē*, often rendered "steadfast endurance"], and patience produces character, and character produces hope" (Rom 5:3-4).

Illness also appears as a source of humility,[74] particularly for those who have not yet reached the heights of the spiritual life. St Diadochus of Photike explains: "As long as the athlete in the realm of piety is at the mid-stage of spiritual experience, it is the infirmities of the body that lead him to develop humility."[75] And in a similar vein, St Nicetas Stethatos writes: "Illnesses are useful to those who are taking their first steps in the virtuous life. They help them exhaust and

---

[69] *On Death* 13-14.
[70] Cf. St Gregory of Nazianzus, *Letters* XXXII.1.
[71] *Letters to Olympiad* IV.2; cf. *Homily on the Paralytic* 1.
[72] *Homily on the Paralytic* 1.
[73] Cf. St John Chrysostom, *Letters to Olympiad* IV.3; St Barsanuphius, *Letters* 189.
[74] Cf. St John Chrysostom, *Homily on Annas* I.2; St John Climacus, *Ladder* XXVI.37; St Symeon the New Theologian, *Catechesis* XXV.158-159.
[75] *One Hundred Chapters* 95; cf. St Nicetas Stethatos, *Centuries* I.87.

humble the burning desires of the flesh. For they weaken the vigor of the flesh and lessen the earthly temptations of the soul."[76]

The suffering that accompanies sickness likewise produces repentance,[77] facilitates compunction,[78] and leaves the soul well disposed toward prayer.[79] These last effects are particularly fruitful, since they essentially motivate all spiritual life.

Nevertheless, we need to be clear about the fact that the purification of passions and the acquisition of virtues, together with various spiritual benefits, are not the effects of sickness itself, nor of the suffering that accompanies it; rather, they are gifts from God bestowed in the framework of illness. Thus, for a person to profit from them, he or she needs to have a proper attitude, that is, to be prepared to receive them, to turn toward God, to open oneself to God's grace, and to strive to assimilate that grace. It is essential that human persons collaborate actively with the divine work, whose purpose is to promote their spiritual progress and salvation.

Sickness constitutes a very real trial.[80] It places the affected person in the situation of Job.[81] For Job is tempted by the devil to curse God, or at least to separate or to distance himself from God by turning into himself in an attitude of pride, or by abandoning himself to various passions which tempt him. Thereby God wants to give him the opportunity to demonstrate the full measure of his commitment to him, and to acquire fully—precisely by means of his efforts to overcome his trials—those virtues which God grants him, in order to unite him more closely with his own divine life.

[76] Centuries I.87.

[77] St John Chrysostom, Homilies on Repentance VII.6.

[78] Cf. St Gregory Palamas, Triads II.2, 6.

[79] Idem.

[80] Cf. St Barsanuphius, Letters 74, 78; St Issac the Syrian, Ascetic Discourses 8.29; St Symeon Metaphrastes, Paraphrase 136.

[81] Cf. St Gregory of Nazianzus, Oration XIV.34; St Barsanuphius, Letters 74.

God's Help and Man's Contribution

To emerge victorious from testing and to enjoy the fruits of victory, a person must first of all avoid passively submitting to the illness and its suffering, and allowing himself to be dominated, enclosed and beaten down by it. To the contrary, it is essential that the person do all possible to preserve a dynamic attitude of vigilance, in expectation of receiving divine assistance. "One should struggle in order not to give in, and then one will receive the help required," St Barsanuphius teaches.[82] And he confesses with regard to a sickness that had previously afflicted him: "Beyond words I was deprived of strength, yet I did not give in; and I continued the struggle until the Lord fortified me."[83]

The ill person should understand that God, at the same time he sends this trial, also furnishes the means to overcome it; above all, he grants the strength needed to resist the temptations of the Enemy. Thus St Barsanuphius offers this counsel: "Let us not give in. We have a merciful God who knows our weakness better than we do; and if, in order to test us, he sends illness, at least we have the Apostle who provides us consolation when he says, "God is faithful, and he will not let you be tempted beyond your strength, but with the temptation will also provide the way of escape, that you may be able to endure it (1 Cor 10:13)."[84] And if God's help is slow in coming, we should know that in any case the trial will not last indefinitely, and that God never leaves a person without a means of help. This is why St Barsanuphius offers the counsel: "Be attentive to the limits of endurance, do not despair and do not be discouraged. For God is near, he who says, 'I will never fail you nor forsake you' (Heb 13:5)."[85]

If God occasionally seems to abandon us, it is only to provide us with the opportunity to be further fortified in faith, hope, patience, and all the other virtues that can manifest themselves in such

---

[82]*Letters* 347.
[83]*Letters* 512; cf. 74.
[84]*Letters* 74.
[85]*Letters* 74; cf. St John of Gaza, *Letters* 79.

circumstances. For this reason, it may even be spiritually more profitable for the ill person not to receive from God an immediate healing. St Barsanuphius confides in one of his spiritual children who had requested that he intercede for the man's healing: "As I began to pray, the Lord said to me, 'Let me test him for the benefit of his soul, even by means of bodily suffering, so that I may know his level of endurance and what reward he should receive in response to his prayers and his pains'."[86]

The ill person should all the more guard himself against discouragement because of the weakness resulting from his state, since that state is by no means a handicap to spiritual struggle. To the contrary, as St Paul teaches, it is in weakness that God manifests his strength. St Barsanuphius affirms the same thing to one of his disciples who is obliged to endure the trials of illness: "Let us not lose courage in illness, for the Apostle said, 'When I am weak, them I am strong' (2 Cor 12:10)."[87]

God watches over the ill person. He protects and helps him, since he is fully aware of the difficulties of his situation. St Isaac the Syrian writes: "God is close to the suffering heart that calls upon him in its affliction. If God does not try him on the level of the body, or if he afflicts him by some other means, nonetheless, because of his love for man, God loves him in his soul to the degree that the suffering with which he is afflicted is difficult."[88] Accordingly, the person burdened with sickness should not be troubled, but should rather "consider the holy strength which comes from above,"[89] abandoning himself with full confidence. According to the counsel of St Barsanuphius: "Since you have God, be not afraid, but place your concern in his hands, and he will take care of you."[90] Even if the illness leads to death, we still need not fear, for as St Paul teaches—in words St Barsanuphius recalls to an ill brother—"If this earthly tent we live in is destroyed,

---

[86]*Letters* 513; cf. St John of Gaza, *Letters* 76, 79, 80.
[87]*Letters* 74.
[88]*Ascetic Discourses* 25.
[89]St John of Gaza, *Letters* 76.
[90]*Letters* 75.

we have a building from God, a house not made with hands, eternal in the heavens" (2 Cor 5:1).[91]

THE IMPORTANCE OF PATIENCE

In the face of the sufferings that afflict him, the ill person should demonstrate above all the virtue of patience. Although this virtue is a gift from God, it can only be acquired through a person's own effort; the person must strive to attain patience, while asking God to grant it to him.

The difficulty with the trials of illness is often due less to the intensity of suffering than to the length to time the illness lasts, together with the discomforts it causes on various levels. It is here, usually, that the demons infiltrate the soul with thoughts of discouragement, sadness, boredom, irritation, annoyance, despair, and revolt. Therefore the Fathers recommend above all attitudes of patience, endurance and steadfastness, referring in this regard to numerous teachings of Christ and the Apostles. St John of Gaza recalled to two of his ill brothers, "the Lord said: 'It is by your steadfastness that you will save your souls' (Lk 21:19). And following him the Apostle said, 'You have need of steadfastness' (Heb 10:36). And the Prophet also declared: 'I waited patiently for the Lord, and he heard me' (Ps 30/40:1). In addition, our sweet Master God said: 'He who endures to the end will be saved' (Mt 10:22). Therefore both of you: remain steadfast in patience!"[92]

St Barsanuphius counseled the same to one of his two brothers: "Let us remain steadfast, let us support one other and be disciples of the Apostle, who said, 'Be patient in tribulation' (Rom 12:12)."[93] And elsewhere he taught that it is essentially through patience that a person demonstrates that illness truly benefits him.[94] Thus he writes to

---

[91]Ibid.
[92]*Letters* 76.
[93]*Letters* 74.
[94]*Letters* 189.

a sick brother: "If you are not steadfast in trials, you will not be able to ascend the cross. But if you first of all endure these trials, you will enter into the harbor of his repose, and from that time on you will live in quietness, unaffected by worries, your soul strengthened and united to the Lord through all things. You will be vigilant in faith, joyous in hope, abounding in charity, and protected by the holy, con-substantial Trinity."[95] And he reveals to us that it is only after having "endured illnesses, fevers and afflictions" that he himself "entered into the harbor of serenity."[96]

THE ESSENTIAL ROLE OF PRAYER

It is chiefly by prayer that an ill person can turn toward God and, by adopting an appropriate attitude, can receive from him the help he needs and the spiritual gifts that can enrich his life.

"Prayer," St Isaac the Syrian writes, "is our strongest help in times of sickness."[97] God never fails to respond to the call made to him in such circumstances, nor to sympathize with the suffering of those who invoke him, St Isaac adds.[98] Yet the help God provides is not always that of healing or of relieving pain. As we pointed out earlier, God gives us what is spiritually the best for us. From this point of view, restoration of health is sometimes beneficial. But sometimes continuation of the illness provides a providential opportunity to receive an even greater benefit.

The saints, enlightened by the Holy Spirit, are well aware of this, requesting in their prayer sometimes relief from suffering and heal-ing, and sometimes virtues which can be acquired or developed through the illness. Thus, for example, St Barsanuphius recounts that his disciple, "Abba Seridos was gravely ill one day, afflicted with a high fever that would not subside. Nevertheless, he did not ask God to heal him or even to lessen his suffering. He asked only that God

---

[95] *Letters* 2; cf. 613.
[96] *Letters* 189.
[97] *Ascetic Discourses* 21.
[98] Ibid.

would grant him endurance and a spirit of thanksgiving."[99] When such discernment is lacking, the ill person should pray that God grant him what is best for him and surrender himself with full confidence to God's will. By systematically requesting that he be healed, the ill person merely seeks the fulfillment of his own will, because the human will always desires the lessening of pain and suffering. Yet a person's illness can also teach him to accept God's will before his own. Through it he can learn to free himself from an egotistical love of self. This is what God might well desire for the patient by delaying his healing, in order to unite that person more intimately to himself by conforming his will to the divine will.

St John Chrysostom notes repeatedly that God's delay in answering our prayer, contrary to what we might at first conclude, in fact represents a sign of his solicitude and of his favor,[100] for God wants to grant us the possibility to manifest—precisely in the period of waiting in which he leaves us—the full range of our virtues.[101] Chrysostom draws our attention to the passage from St Matthew's gospel (15:21-32) where we see Christ several times reject the prayers the Canaanite woman addresses to him (as he does those addressed by the Apostles), before he accords healing to her sick daughter. Yet just afterwards he immediately heals a crowd of sick persons who are simply placed at his feet. St John notes: "He answers the petition of the Canaanite woman only after he has several times rejected her request; yet on the contrary, he heals all these sick people the moment they present themselves to him." And he explains Christ's way of responding to each situation by referring to the paradoxical character of each: "It is not at all because the crowd of sick people were preferable to the Canaanite woman, but because this woman had more faith than all of them put together. By putting off the healing, Jesus Christ wanted to reveal to others her generosity and faithfulness."[102]

---

[99]*Letters* 570 ter.
[100]Cf. *Homilies on Repentance* III.4; *Homilies on Genesis* XXX.5-6; XLIX.1; *Homily on Holy Week* 5-6; *Homilies on Matthew* XXIII.4, LII.3; *Homilies on Ephesians* XXIV.3.
[101]Ibid.
[102]*Homilies on Matthew* LII.3.

Far from being a source of despair and a reason for abandoning prayer, the fact that we are not immediately healed in response to our request should be taken as a reason to hope in still greater benefits and, consequently, it should serve as a motivation toward greater perseverance in our petition.

It is above all by means of prayer that man unites himself with God, opens himself to the grace that God ceaselessly bestows, and receives from him every aid, strength and blessing. For this reason, prayer should be the ill person's chief activity. During the illness of his disciple Dositheus, St Dorotheus of Gaza was preoccupied above all to know if the younger monk was able to remain steadfast in prayer. "When he was ill, Dorotheus said to him, 'Dositheus, be attentive to prayer; be watchful, so that you do not lose it.' And Dositheus replied, 'Very well, my lord, then pray for me!' Again when the disciple was somewhat beaten down by trials, Dorotheus asked him, 'So, Dositheus, how is your prayer? Is it still there?' And Dositheus replied, 'Yes, my lord, thanks to your prayers'."[103]

Prayer during illness, however, should not be limited to requests; it should also include thanksgiving. The Fathers insist above all on this latter aspect.[104] They base this admonition on a word of St Paul to which they return repeatedly: "Give thanks in all circumstances; for this is the will of God in Christ Jesus for you" (1 Thess 5:18). The prayer of thanksgiving consists on the one hand in thanking God for his blessings in general as for this particular circumstance of illness, and on the other hand in praising him.[105] Christ himself teaches us that thanksgiving should be for a person the ultimate end of their illness, and that every illness should be used to glorify God. Regarding the illness of Lazarus he says: "This illness is not unto death; it is for the glory of God, so that the Son of God may be glorified by means of it" (Jn 11:4). This word applies equally to everyone who finds himself or herself in the same position as Lazarus. It can be understood

---

[103] *Life of St Dositheus* 10.

[104] See, for example, St Barsanuphius, *Letters* 2, 72, 74-78, 189, 510, 515, 570 ter.; St John of Gaza, *Letters* 76, 80, 123, 384; St Isaac the Syrian, *Ascetic Discourses* 5.

[105] Cf. Origen, *On Prayer* 14.33; St John Cassian, *Conferences* IX.14, 15.

in this way: the illness of the body does not bring about the death of the soul, nor does it cause the ultimate death of the body; it ought to be used by the person to celebrate the glory of God and of his Son, who came in the Father's name to bring healing to every human affliction. A second interpretation of this passage is also possible and serves merely to confirm the first: by the healing of this illness and of the death which it can bring about, God manifests his power in the person of his Son, in whom and by whom we are called to glorify God. We can understand in the same way this other teaching of Christ in connection with the man born blind: this man was born with his infirmity "in order that the works of God might be made manifest in him" (Jn 9:3). The "works of God" include the healing of soul and body effected by Christ, but they also refer to the celebration of God made possible in and through every illness and every infirmity.

Prayer in all of its forms can enable the ill person, whose spirit is focused on God, to transcend suffering to the point that they no longer experience it. St Barsanuphius writes to a sick brother, "If your spirit was where it should be, even the bites of poisonous snakes and scorpions would not be able to make you feel physical suffering."[106] And Palladius cites the case of Stephen the Libyan who, when operated on wide awake and in an area of the body that is particularly sensitive, was totally unaffected by pain: "He acted as if it were someone else who was experiencing the operation. Although his members were completely amputated, he appeared to be as free from pain as if someone were merely cutting his hair. He was powerfully supported by the grace of God."[107] But such cases, in which the soul appears to be totally independent of the body to which it is joined, are of course rare. The spiritual destiny of most people—including most saints—consists rather in having to assume their suffering in God.

At times pain is so great that it deprives a person of all the strength needed to persevere in prayer, and prayer can no longer be exercised in its usual forms. In such cases, the ill person can only

---

[106]*Letters* 514.
[107]*Lausiac History* XXIV.2.

remain in silence in the presence of God, reaching out to him with the little strength he has left, to unite himself inwardly with him. "When St Dositheus was further afflicted—he was so weak that he had to be carried about in a sheet—Dorotheus said to him: 'How is your prayer, Dositheus?' He replied, 'Forgive me, I no longer have the strength to pray.' 'Don't worry, then, about prayer,' the elder answered him, 'just guard the memory of God and know that he is with you.'"[108]

The conscious mind often obsesses in cases of extreme suffering, to the point that it can confound the faculties of the soul. Then we can do nothing other than to accept this state of utter emptiness, of personal barrenness, in an attitude of total abandonment of the self into the hands of God, in imitation of the crucified Christ: "Father, into thy hands I commit my spirit" (Lk 23:46). Such an act of self-abandonment is made neither by words nor by thoughts, but in the depths of the heart. Lived out in God, the misery of both body and soul become a form of spiritual poverty. Whatever we lack at such moments, Christ supplies to us: what we cannot utter in such moments, the Holy Spirit utters for us: "Abba, Father!" (Rom 8:15).

The Way of Holiness

Among all the attitudes recommended by the Fathers in times of illness, patience and thanksgiving come first.[109] "St John of Gaza goes so far as to affirm that "God demands of the sick person nothing other than thanksgiving and endurance."[110] By these two dispositions of the soul, the patient can realize one of the highest forms of ascetic practice and a truly spiritual pathway. "Such is the greatest form of asceticism," Amma Syncletica teaches, "that we master ourselves in times of illness, addressing to God hymns of thanksgiving."[111] The

---

[108] Life of St Dositheus 10.
[109] St Barsanuphius, Letters 2, 72, 74, 189, 512, 613, 770; St John of Gaza, Letters 76, 80.
[110] Letters 123.
[111] Apophthegmata, alph. series, Syncletica 10.

Fathers celebrate both of these virtues, stressing the power they possess to lead the ill person to the highest summits of the spiritual life and to grant him salvation.

With regard to patience, St John Cassian writes: "The advantage that illness can sometimes present appears quite clearly with the beatitude illustrated by the poor, ulcerated Lazarus. Scripture makes no mention at all in his regard of any virtue. His great patience in supporting his poverty and illness alone merits the blessed fortune to be admitted into the bosom of Abraham."[112] Referring to this same parable, St John Chrysostom likewise underscores the fact that Lazarus did nothing extraordinary other than suffer his illness and his poverty with patience, and it is this that earned him eternal salvation.[113] For his part, St Macarius affirms that "when souls have been delivered from various afflictions—whether these be caused by other people, or they result from bodily illnesses—they receive the same crowns and the same assurance as the martyrs, if they have preserved patience until the end."[114]

As for thanksgiving, St Diadocus of Photike writes: "If [the soul] receives with thanksgiving the pains provoked by illness, it demonstrates that it is not far from the boundaries of impassibility."[115] And Abba Poemen does not hesitate to declare: "If three men meet, and one preserves interior peace, the second gives thanks to God in illness, and the third serves with purity of thought, these three accomplish the same work."[116]

It is for this reason that St Gregory of Nazianzus urges us to have a great deal of respect and veneration for those who are ill, since some of them, by virtue of their trials and tribulations, will attain sanctity: "Let us respect the illness that accompanies sanctity and offer homage to those whose sufferings have led to victory; for it may be that among these ill persons there is hidden another Job."[117]

---

[112] *Conferences* VI.3.
[113] *Letters to Olympiad* IV.3.
[114] St Symeon Metaphrastes, *Paraphrase* 131.
[115] *One Hundred Chapters* 54.
[116] *Apophthegmata*, alph. series, Poemen 29.
[117] *Oration* XXIV.34.

3.
Christian Paths toward Healing

SEEK HEALING TO GLORIFY GOD

If sickness and suffering can and should be spiritually transcended and transfigured in Christ, and if they can constitute an ascetic pathway capable of leading the ill person to spiritual heights, nevertheless they should never be either desired or sought after. This is because they require of us a great deal of strength that is lost in vain through the struggles of the body. It would be far more preferable that the energy which is spent in this fashion be used in the exercise of the commandments[1] and in praise of God. For such holy works demand strength beyond measure, and the strength we have when we are in good health is minimal by comparison with what is really needed for us to celebrate the infinite glory of the Thrice-Holy God.

While from a certain point of view illnesses can be of aid to the spiritual life, from another, they are merely an obstacle, as St Nicholas Stethatos insists: "As much as [sickness] is useful to beginners, to the same degree it harms those who are more advanced in the struggles toward virtue. They effectively hinder them from giving themselves over wholly to the affairs of God, they limit the soul's reflectiveness because of pain and affliction, they trouble the soul by placing it under a cloud of discouragement, and they undermine contrition by rendering their thoughts dry and sterile."[2]

It goes without saying that health ought to be preferred to sickness, on condition, nevertheless, that it is lived in God and for God.

---

[1]Therefore St Thalassios recommends: "Treat your body as a servant of the commandments, preserving it as much as you can from all illness" (*Centuries* II.81).

[2]*Centuries* I.87.

It is not out of mere politeness that holy people, following the apostle John (3 Jn 2), wish good health to their visitors or correspondents, nor that the Church, in all of its liturgical services, asks God to preserve or reestablish the health of all its members.

The Gospels clearly indicate that the reason a return to health is to be desired is primarily spiritual. In the episode in which Christ heals Peter's mother-in-law, it is stated that "the fever left her. She arose and *served him*" (Mt 8:15). And in the healing of the paralytic it is noted that "he rose before them, and took up that on which he lay, *and went home, glorifying God*" (Lk 5:25). The same point is repeatedly stressed in administration of the sacrament of Holy Unction or Anointing of the Sick: "You who heal and help those who are in pain, the Liberator and Savior of the sick, Master and Lord of all things, grant healing to your ill servant . . . *so that he/she might glorify your divine power*";[3] "grant him/her the healing of soul and body, *that he might praise you with love and glorify your strength*";[4] "Hasten to visit your suffering servants, deliver them from their illnesses and raise them up from their bitter suffering, *that they might ceaselessly hymn and praise you*";[5] "O Lord, send down from heaven your healing Power, touch this body, calm its fever, put an end to its suffering and every hidden weakness. Be the physician of this, your servant, raise him/her up from this bed of pain and suffering, and *restore him/her safe and sound to your Church, well-pleasing to you and able to fulfill your calling*";[6] "Drive far from him/her all sickness and infirmity, so that, raised up by your powerful hand, *he/she might serve you and offer you unceasing thanks*";[7] "Holy Father, physician of souls and bodies, who has sent your only Son our Lord Jesus Christ to heal every sickness and to deliver us from death, heal your servant (N.) from the infirmities of body and soul which possess him/her, and enliven him/her through the grace of your Christ, and preserve the life of this person

---

[3]Canon, Ode 3.
[4]Verse from the Praises.
[5]Troparion.
[6]Prayer of the third unction.
[7]Prayer of the fourth unction.

who, according to your good pleasure and by his good works will render to you the thanksgiving which is due."[8]

Under these conditions, the quest for healing even appears to be the Christian's duty, as St Isaac the Syrian notes: "He who is ill and knows his illness owes it to himself to ask for healing."[9]

In addition to the fact that it hinders a person from mobilizing for God all the strength and capacity that he has been given, illness remains a disorder and even a negation of human nature as God created it in the beginning, and as the incarnate Word restored it in his person as the enfleshed Logos. By its very origins illness remains linked to evil, to the "powers of darkness," of destruction and death, that is, to the sin of Adam and to the subsequent corruption of human nature in its entirety.[10] Rather than accept and give in to illness in a fatalistic way, the human person, benefiting from the victory obtained by the God-man over sin and the forces of evil, should do everything within his power to combat it. This struggle against illness indirectly constitutes a part of the larger struggle one is called to assume against the powers of evil. In this regard, Theodoret of Cyrus makes judicious use of a military metaphor: "Those who suffer the assaults of illness strive to drive away the sickness of their body as they would drive away their enemies."[11]

CHRIST THE PHYSICIAN

Christ, who dwelt among men to heal them of their spiritual ills, never hesitated to ease from their bodily illness and infirmities those who requested healing from him. He did not see in such sufferings any *necessary* affliction. Far from being resigned or indifferent in the face of illness, Christ revealed clearly, by healing those who came to him, that illness is undesirable. And he gave an example of the attitude to be adopted when it occurs.

---

[8]Prayer at every unction.
[9]*Ascetic Discourses* 3.
[10]Cf. chapter one.
[11]*Discourse on Providence* III.

Nor did he hesitate to present himself as a physician: "Those who are well have no need of a physician, but those who are sick" (Mt 9:12; Mk 2:17; Lk 7:31); "Doubtless you will quote to me this proverb, 'Physician, heal yourself'" (Lk 4:23). And the multitude of healings that he worked—which the Gospels take pains to relate in detail— bear witness to the fact that he meant by his actions to be a physician not only of souls but also of bodies.

Significantly, it is after having recalled an episode in which Christ exorcised spirits and healed the illnesses of those brought to him that St Matthew recalls Isaiah's prophecy, "He took our infirmities and bore our diseases" (Mt 8:16-17; Is 53:5). It is precisely as the physician of bodies that Jesus appears to many of those who knew him during his earthly life: his adversaries—who accused him above all of work-ing a healing on the Sabbath (Mt 12:10; Lk 6:7; Mk 3:2)—but also those in the large crowds who drew near to him to receive healing of their physical illnesses and infirmities.

At the beginning of the Christian era, Christ was often favorably compared to Asclepius, the healing god of pagan Greek and Roman cults.[12] The first Christian apologists actually preserved this compar-ison for a while,[13] for didactic reasons, taking care, of course, to insist that Christ is the only true Physician, whereas Asclepius was nothing but an idol[14] or a demon.[15] This function as physician of bodies, ful-filled by Christ and then in his name by the apostles, is so striking that the pagan observers described Christianity as a religion "for the sick."[16] Their surprise was due to the fact that at this period religions tended to despise sick people and seek their followers from among the healthy.[17]

---

[12]See the article by T.L. Robinson, "Asclepius, Cult of," in *The Anchor Bible Dic-tionary*, vol. I (New York: Doubleday, 1992), 475-476. Also H. Leclercq, "Médecins," *Dictionnaire d'archéologie et de liturgie* XI, vol. I (Paris, 1933), col. 158.

[13]Cf., for example, St Justin, *First Apology* 22.

[14]Clement of Alexandria, *Protrepticus* 29.1; 52.4.

[15]Tertullian, *Apologeticum* 23.6-7; Origen, *Contra Celsum* III.24.

[16]Cf. P. Lain Entralgo, *Maladie et culpabilité* (Paris, 1970), p. 75.

[17]A. Harnack, "Medicinisches aus der ältesten Kirchengeschichte," *Texte und Untersuchungen* VIII.4 (Leipzig, 1892), p. 128.

These represent distortions of early Christianity, however, in that they tend to limit their perspective so as to see in Jesus Christ a mere healer of bodily ills and to assimilate him to the mass of magicians and healers found in this period.[18] Thereby they failed to grasp the fact that he is equally the physician of souls. But an equal distortion would be to see him as concerned only with spiritual healing. Consequently, in order to show that it is the whole person Christ came to heal and to save, the Fathers and the entire Tradition of the Church are careful to present him as both "Physician of bodies"[19] and "Physician of souls."[20] Their concern is to stress the unity characteristic of the human person and the common destiny of both soul and body of each individual. Accordingly, they most frequently call Christ by the title "Physician of the soul and body."[21]

---

[18]Cf. Origen, *Contra Celsum* I.68.

[19]See esp. Clement of Alexandria, *Paidagogos* I.6.2-3; St Athanasius of Alexandria, *On the Incarnation of the Word* XVIII; St Cyril of Jerusalem, *Baptismal Catechism* X.13.

[20]In this regard see our study, *Thérapeutique des maladies spirituelles* (Paris, 1991), t. I, part 3, ch. I, pp. 319-344, on "Christ the Physician," with numerous patristic references.

[21]See esp. St Ignatius of Antioch, *To the Ephesians* VII.1-2; Clement of Alexandria, *Paidagogos* I.6.2: "Our good Pedagogue, he who is the Wisdom and Word of the Father and who created man, is concerned with his creature as a totality; he heals both body and soul, being the Physician of humanity and capable of healing all things." Cf. St Cyril of Jerusalem, *Baptismal Catechism* X.13: "In the Greek language, 'Jesus' signifies 'healer.' For he is the Physician of bodies and souls." And St John Chrysostom, *Homilies on the demons* I.5: "God is the true Physician, the unique Physician of body and soul." *Homily on Genesis*, 27; *Hom. On Mt* 29:2. Theodoret of Cyrus, *History of the Syrian Monks*, 14.3. St Barsanuphius, *Letters* 107: "The Lord be with you, he who is the great physician of souls and bodies"; 199: "Jesus is the physician of souls and bodies." St Symeon the New Theologian, *Ethical Discourses* 7, 267-268: we call on him who is the physician of souls and bodies." On the "Christ Physician," one may see A. Harnack, *op. cit.* K. Knur, *Christus medicus?* (Fribourg-im-Brisgau, 1905). J. Ott, "Die Bezeichnung Christi als *iatros* in der urchristlichen Literatur," *Der Katholik*, 90, 1910, 454-458. H. Shipperges, "zur tradition des 'Christus Medicus' im frühen Christentum und in der älteren Heilkunde," *Arzt Christi*, 11, 1965, 12-20. G. Dumeige, "Le Christ médecin dans la littérature chrétienne des premiers siècles," *Rivista di archeologia christiana* 48, 1972, 115-141; "(Christ) Médecin," *Dictionnaire de Spiritualité*, t. X, col. 891-901. J.-C. Larchet, *Thérapeutiques des maladies spirituelles* (Paris, 1991), t. I, 3è partie, chap. I, 319-44, "Le Christ Médecin."

THE SAINTS HEAL IN THE NAME OF CHRIST

Having called his twelve disciples, Christ conferred his healing power upon them: he made them physicians like himself, giving them power to command and cast out evil spirits (Mk 6:7; Lk 9:1) as well as to heal any illness or infirmity (Mk 10:1, 8; Lk 9:2. Cf. Mk 6:13 and Lk 9:6). After the apostles, this healing power was conveyed to all those who, through a divine-human asceticism, became like Christ. They are the holy "godbearers" whose *Lives* attest to the many healings they performed and who, like him, would be called "physicians."

Nevertheless, Christ is "the only physician,"[22] for through the Apostles and the saints it is always he who heals:[23] they are able to heal only in his name and deem themselves to be mere mediators. Thus the holy Apostle Peter says to the crowd that has come to see him perform a miraculous healing: "why do you stare at us, as though by our own power or piety we had made him walk? ... faith in [Jesus'] name has made this man strong whom you see and know" (Acts 3:12, 16). And St Athanasius the Great has this to say about Antony: "Through him the Lord heals many."[24] Theodoret of Cyrus expresses a similar thought with regard to the monk-healers whose lives he presents: "Those who have been initiated into the mysteries of the Spirit know the generosity of the Spirit and what miracles he has wrought in man through man."[25] Then St Athanasius tells us that when St Antony performed a healing, "he always gave thanks to the Lord. He reminded those who were ill that the healing was neither his nor anyone's, but that it was God's alone ... Thus the sick learned to give thanks not to Antony but only to God."[26] St Antony himself says: "I do not have this power to heal ... healing is the work of the Lord. In every place he has mercy on those who call on him. The

---

[22] St Ignatius of Antioch, *Ephesians* VII.2. Clement of Alexandria, *Paidagogos* I.6.1. St John Chrysostom, *Homily on the demons* I.5.

[23] Cf. St John Chrysostom, *Treatise on Repentance,* II.9.

[24] *Life of Antony* 14.

[25] *History of the Monks of Syria,* Prologue, 10. Cf. II.6, an addition to the Syriac version: "another wonder of the Blessed One, which our Lord Jesus Christ did through the hands of the Blessed One ..."

[26] *Life of Antony* 56. Cf. Theodoret, *op. cit.,* 26.6.

Lord has heard my prayer and he has made known his love for mankind by revealing to me that he would heal . . ."[27]

Such assertions are necessary in the event of a healing because men tend to give glory to the healer rather than to God. The people of Lystra did so with Paul and Barnabas, saying of them: "The gods have come down to us in the likeness of men," calling them Zeus and Hermes and attempting to offer them sacrifices (Acts 14:8-13). The two Apostles had great difficulty getting them to admit that they were also men of the same nature, and exhorted them to turn "to a living God" (Acts 14:15). It is to avoid just such a confusion, and so that none of the healings performed by the power of God would be attributed directly to them, that the holy healers, in their humility, often have recourse to material means. They perform rites or give strange prescriptions that most often have no therapeutic value in themselves, but serve to divert the attention and the gratitude of those whom they heal so that these might turn more easily and more completely to the One who is the only source of healing.

Out of faithfulness to Christ, his apostles and his saints, Christians have always focused their efforts on caring for and healing the sick either through specifically religious therapeutic methods, or through secular medicine to which they nevertheless attribute a new, spiritual meaning. But since Christ is truly "the only physician of the body," these diverse therapeutic methods are simply, as we shall see, various means which he provides for us to ask for, convey and receive his grace: the energies which he has from the Father and gives to mankind through the Spirit, either directly, or indirectly through the works of creation.

Spiritual Paths Toward Healing

Prayer

Prayer is the first among all the religious healing arts because it is the foundation and a necessary element of all the others, and because it

---

[27]*Life of Antony* 58. Cf. Callinicos, *Life of Hypatios* 9.8. Theodoret, *op. cit.*, 9.7.

is uniquely efficacious in combating illness.[28] "Is any one among you suffering? Let him pray," says the Apostle James (5:13), that he may patiently bear his illness, but that he may also be delivered from it. May he invoke the help of the "great and heavenly physician," crying out like the blind man in Jericho: "Jesus, Son of David, have mercy on me!" (Lk 18:38). In so doing he will open himself up to the regenerative power of divine grace.

In order to grant him the desired healing, God asks of man only one thing: that he pray to him in faith. Jesus asked the two blind men: "Do you believe that I am able to do this?" (Mt 9:28). What one receives from God is according to the measure of one's faith. "Be it done for you as you have believed," said Christ to the centurion. And to the woman with the flow of blood (Mt 9:22; Mk 5:34; Lk 8:48) as to the sinful woman (Lk 7:50), the blind man (Mk 10:52) and the leper (Lk 17:19) he said: "Your faith has made you well."[29] For the grace of God rests on all mankind—and in fullness upon those who are baptized. In order to receive it one need only face it and be open to it. This is why Christ said: "Whatever you ask in prayer, believe that you receive it and you will" (Mk 11:24). To one who asks with an unfailing faith (Lk 22:32) and without doubting (Mt 21:21), God gives all things according to his promise: "Whatever you ask in prayer, you will receive, if you have faith" (Mt 21:22). We also know, however, that while some have received according to their faith, the requests of many others have remained unanswered: "And there were many lepers in Israel in the time of the prophet Elisha; and none of them was cleansed, but only Naaman the Syrian" (Lk 4:27).

Praying for One's Neighbor

Knowing that we are weak and slow to believe (cf. Lk 24:25), St Paul admonishes us all to "bear one another's burdens" (Gal 6:12). And St Cyril of Jerusalem has said that "there is such power in faith that the believer is not saved alone but rather some have been saved through

---

[28]Cf., for example, St John Chrysostom, *Homilies Against the Anomeans* V.6.
[29]See also Mt 5:36; 8:10; 15:28; Lk 7:9; 8:50; 18:42; Jn 9:35.

the faith of others."[30] The fact that a person can be healed through the prayers of another, or those of many, is clearly revealed in the gospels through the example of the paralytic: Christ heals not when he sees this man's faith but when he sees the faith of those who brought him (Mt 9:2; Mk 2:5; Lk 5:20). A Christian, therefore, must pray not simply to receive healing for himself, but also for the health of his ailing brothers, "for by one Spirit we were all baptized into one body . . . and all were made to drink of one Spirit" (1 Cor 12:13). And again, "God has so adjusted the body, giving the greater honor to the inferior part, that there may be no discord in the body, but that the members may have the same care for one another. If one member suffers, all suffer together" (1 Cor 12:24-26). Through this solidarity and this unity of the members, it is no longer one person, in his weakness and his limitations, who prays to God, but many—and one might say all—by virtue of the communion of saints which, within the Church, is realized in Christ through the Spirit.

Furthermore, this communal prayer has great power because it is that of the whole body, which is the body of Christ (cf. 1 Cor 12:27), in which the Spirit confers upon men the grace that comes from the Father. Thus Christ says: "If two of you agree on earth about anything they ask, it will be done for them by my Father in heaven. For where two or three are gathered in my name, there am I in the midst of them" (Mt 18:19-20). God makes himself present not only because the unity of these members constitutes the ecclesial community, but also because it manifests the bond of love through which, within this community, mankind is united to God and God to mankind: "If we love one another, God abides in us" (1 Jn 4:12). "God is love, and he who abides in love abides in God, and God abides in him" (1 Jn 4:16). Likewise it would seem that communal prayer is the form best-suited for obtaining the healing grace of God. As St James says: "Pray for one another, that you may be healed" (5:16).

And so praying for the healing of one's neighbor comes to be part of the spiritual responsibility of every Christian, as a means of fulfilling the second great commandment: "You shall love your neighbor as

---

[30]*Baptismal Catechism* 5.8.

yourself" (Mt 22:39; Mk 12:31). In these words the whole law is summed up (Rom 13:8-10). This prayer is a way through which man aligns himself with God in his great compassion for all suffering creatures. When it is unceasing and deep, it becomes a sign of holiness.[31]

The Prayer of the Saints

When a saint is moved by his love for those whose suffering he shares and by his desire to relieve them of it, he is able to reach up to God with a pure and unfailing prayer, because he has purified himself of every passion through a divine-human asceticism.[32] Furthermore, his own voice, among all others, is especially efficacious, according to St James: "The prayer of a righteous man has great power in its effects" (Jas 5:16). That is why Christians, when they wish to receive healing from God, ask for the intercessions of their spiritual elders: the *Lives* of saints show them endlessly receiving visitors who come asking for their help. And to this same end all the saints pray "who at all times have been well-pleasing unto God." The first is the Mother of God, "the fervent intercessor before the Creator" who, because she gave birth to the Word of God in the flesh, has the greatest power of any intercessor before her Son.

Nevertheless, while healing grace is always from God, who is the only source of all grace, it is not something external to the saints who convey it to mankind. The saint prays and gives thanks for this gift which God gives him, and through him to mankind. Yet he himself bears it and possesses it (yet without appropriating it). He has this power at his disposal (though always aligning his will with that of God) in order to benefit those who call on him, and he does so to the measure of his own sanctification. "God often endows the souls of the saints with the charisms of the Spirit," says Theodoret of Cyrus.[33] The more man frees himself from his passions and lives virtuously by

---

[31]Cf. St Mark the Hermit, *Controversy with a Lawyer* 20. St Isaac the Syrian, *Ascetical Homilies* 81.

[32]Cf. St John Chrysostom, *Homélies contre les Anoméens* V.6.

[33]*History of the Monks of Syria*, Prologue, 10.

following the commandments, the more he becomes like God, in Christ and through the Holy Spirit. He becomes more and more suffused with the divine energies that make him a "participant in the divine nature" (2 Pet 1:4), and thus in the Power of God (cf. Eph 1:19). Thereby, according to Christ's own words, he is able to act as God does: "He who believes in me shall do the works that I do" (Jn 14:12). This is why we address the saints not simply as intercessors and intermediaries but also as having within themselves the power to heal. They can do so because they have been deified through grace and have become participants in divine Life and Power. We pray especially to the Mother of God, the first human being to have been fully deified and glorified, "the comfort of the afflicted and the healing of the sick," "the hope of the hopeless," "the strength of those who are struggling," "unquenchable and inexhaustible treasure of healing,"[34] "from whom marvels spring forth and healing flows out."[35]

As they bear divine energies within their entire being, the saints often convey them to those who, in faith, touch their body (cf. Acts 20:9-10), or their clothes (cf. Acts 19:12), or even their shadow (cf. Acts 5:15). After leaving this world, they continue to convey these energies to those who call upon them. They may do so directly or indirectly by means of their relics[36] which are suffused with and radiate these energies, or through their icons which are their visible manifestations, representations of their deified humanity that bring into contact with them those who venerate them. Many sanctuaries where miraculous icons and relics are found become places of pilgrimage where many faithful have found—and still find—healing.

The Charism of Healing: Its Nature and Limits

While in the case of holiness, the power to heal appears to be a

---

[34]Lesser and Great Canon Paraclytique.
[35]Service of Holy Unction.
[36]Cf., for example, Palladius, *Lausiac History* XXXVII.12. *Life of Athanasius the Athonite* 55. *Collection grecque de miracles*, ed. and trans., A.J. Festugière (Paris, 1971), passim.

charism based on a certain level of spiritual perfection,[37] we may note
that in early Christianity, many had the gift of healing, as well as the
gifts of prophecy and of speaking in tongues, although these were not
considered signs of their holiness. St John Chrysostom comments on
this, going so far as to say that "those who received these gifts of old
were not worthy of them! These healers led corrupt lives and, though
rich with the gifts of God, they did not take it upon themselves to
perfect their own lives."[38] We may wonder at the reason for the pro-
liferation of such charisms which, shortly thereafter, declined considerably. St John Chrysostom affirms that if the baptized faithful of his
time had lived in the age of nascent Christianity, they too could have
manifested such gifts.[39] If an entire assembly of Christians had them
then, "it is because the doctrine of salvation had to be widely dissem-
inated, because it was the first age and the beginning of the new religion."[40] The people of that period, he explains, "were taken with and
admired only corporeal things; they were incapable of understanding
a good thing which was not corporeal; they could not conceive of a
spiritual grace that can be apprehended only through the eyes of
faith; this is why there were signs . . . to convince the non-believers."[41]
The saints of that time, however, were too few to make these signs
known, and many more of the baptized faithful needed to be invested
with this mission, regardless of their level of spiritual perfection. But
as men learned to separate their faith from these signs, there came to
be fewer of them.[42] God "wanted to show us that our faith is separate
from guarantees and signs,"[43] because the more striking the events

---

[37]One example of this type of healing can be found already in the Old Testa-
ment, in 2 Kg 13:20-21. Cf. Callinicos, *Life of Hypatios* IX.9; XII.2. Palladius, *Lausiac
History* XII.1; XVII.2; XXXIX.4; XLII. Theodoret of Cyrus, *History of the Monks of
Syria* I.3. See also H. Weinel, *Die Wirkungen des Geistes und der Geister in nachapos-
tolischer Zeitalter bis auf Irenäus* (Fribourg-im-Brisgau, 1899), t. II, pp. 109-127,
"Heilungen und Wunder."

[38]*Homilies on Acts* II.3.

[39]*Homilies on Pentecost* I.4. Cf. Nicholas Cabasilas, *Life in Christ* III.9.

[40]*Homilies on Acts* II.3.

[41]*Homilies on Pentecost* I.4.

[42]Ibid.

[43]Ibid. Cf. *Homilies on Colossians* IX.5.

are and the more they impress themselves on our minds, the smaller our faith becomes." In the face of overwhelming evidence, the believer can no longer have faith.[44] Far from betraying a decadence of spiritual life, the paucity of signs appears instead as a deeper expression of it, as faith must then find a deeper inner foundation.[45] Together with St John Chrysostom we may note, however, that while "the primary purpose of healings is holiness" and the second is "the edification of the Church," there is a third: "to reward the faith either of those who offer up these illnesses, or of those who are themselves ill." This reason, like the one before it, would explain why the power of healing might come "even from sinners and those who are unworthy."[46]

Holy Unction

There are other practices in addition to prayer—though always based on prayer—whose purpose is to invoke and effect the healing grace of God.

The first to mention is holy unction. This practice is attested to in the Gospels and many of the healings by the Apostles are connected to it: "they . . . anointed with oil many that were sick and healed them," says the evangelist Mark (6:13). Meanwhile, the Apostle James recommends its ecclesiastical usage in the following way: "Is any among you sick? Let him call for the elders of the church, and let them pray over him, anointing him with oil in the name of the Lord; and the prayer of faith will save the sick man, and the Lord will raise him up; and if he has committed sins, he will be forgiven" (Jas 5:14-15).

The Orthodox Church continues this apostolic practice by conferring the sacrament of holy unction not only on the dying but upon

---

[44]*Homilies on 1 Corinthians* VI.3.

[45]Cf. *Homilies on Pentecost* I.4; *Homilies on Acts* IV.7-8. Origen, *Adv. Celsus* II.48. This does not mean that the number of healings has since diminished, but that these have to a large degree ceased to be visible and widely known, and no longer serve as signs.

[46]*Conferences* XV.1.

all the sick who ask for it, even if their illness does not seem in any way severe. In its usual form it is administered by seven priests, the elders (*presbyteroi*) of the Church referred to by the Apostle James. The service is made up of three long sections.[47] The first part is a "service of consolation" (*paraklesis*) for the one about to receive the sacrament. The second part centers on the blessing of the holy oil to be used for the anointings. After having prayed "for the blessing of this oil through the power, the action and the descent of the Holy Spirit," the seven priests, each in turn, say the following prayer: "O Lord who, in thy mercy and compassion, healest the torments of our souls and bodies, thou thyself, O Master, sanctify this oil that it may be a healing for those who are anointed with it and an end to all suffering, to every physical and spiritual infirmity and to all evil . . ."The third part consists of the anointing of the sick by each of the priests. Each unction is preceded by readings from the epistles and from the Gospels.[48] These fourteen readings represent the main passages of Scripture having to do with healing as seen both from the perspective of the sick person and from that of those around them. After the readings, the priest who is about to perform the unction says a prayer. These seven prayers constitute the fundamental core of the service. Bringing to mind the mercy and compassion which God has always shown mankind, they ask him to preserve the life of the sick person, to alleviate his suffering, and to heal and strengthen his body. Most importantly, they ask God to forgive his sins, to confirm his spiritual life, to assure his salvation and sanctification, and to accomplish the regeneration of his entire being and the renewal of his life in Christ. Each prayer puts special emphasis on one or the other of these

---

[47]A detailed description can be found together with the complete text of the service in Mercenier, *La prière des Eglises de rite Byzantin*, t. I, 2nd ed., Chevetogne, 1937, pp. 417-446. If it is not possible to gather seven priests, three, two, or even one may perform the rite. When necessary, an abbreviated form of the service also exists (cf., ibid., pp. 246-247).

[48]Before the first unction: Jas 5:10-16 and Lk 10:25-37; before the second: Rom 15:1-7 and Lk 19:1-10; before the third: 1 Cor 12:27-13:8 and Mt 10:1, 5, 8; before the fourth: 2 Cor 6:16-7:1 and Mt 8:14-23; before the fifth: 2 Cor 1:8-11 and Mt 25:1-13; before the sixth: Gal 5:22-6:2 and Mt 15:21-28; before the seventh: 1 Thess 5:14-23 and Mt 9:9-13.

elements, but all of them connect the consolation of the soul with that of the body, spiritual healing with physical healing, and they emphasize the fundamental importance of the former without underestimating that of the latter. Then follows the unction, together with the prayer: "O holy Father, physician of our souls and bodies, who hast sent thine only Son, our Lord Jesus Christ, to heal all evil and to free us from death, deliver also thy servant N . . . from his weaknesses both physical and spiritual, through the grace of thy Christ, and preserve the life of this man . . . for thou art the fountain of healing, O our God, and we ascribe glory to thee and to thine only Son and to thy consubstantial Spirit, now and ever and unto ages of ages." Then the seven priests together place the open Gospel Book on the head of the sick person and recite a penitential prayer asking God for the forgiveness of his sins. In fact the entire service bears a strong penitential character. The main reason for this is that the aim of this sacrament is not merely physical healing but also the healing of spiritual illness and the forgiveness of sins. This is consistent with the prescription of St James and the double meaning of the verb *sōzein*: ". . . the prayer of faith will heal/save the sick man, and the Lord will raise him up; and if he has committed sins, he will be forgiven" (5:15). This penitential aspect is further justified by the fact that every bodily illness is rooted in sin (even though this is not always a personal sin, as St James emphasizes through the use of the conditional conjunction *kan*: "and *if* he has committed sins . . ."), and that healing necessarily entails the destruction of sin and the restoration of our fallen nature. Finally, it is justified by the fact that a return to physical health truly has meaning, as we will see further, only in relation to mankind's ultimate end, to the salvation of his whole being which is made possible only through a victory over sin. It is from this perspective that the Church, throughout the service, asks God for the salvation of the sick as well as for the healing of his physical illness.[49]

---

[49]For these same reasons the sacrament may be received by anyone who, though he may be physically healthy, wishes to be healed spiritually. This is why the Russian Church administers it to all the faithful during Holy Week. In the Greek Church, it is commonly served in families and in the absence of any physical illness, while several ancient *euchologia* prescribe unction for anyone in attendance.

It is notable that anointing with holy oil is not practiced strictly in a sacramental setting. Many spiritual elders use it freely, while the *Lives* of saints tell of numerous healings effected in this way.[50]

The Use of Holy Water

Another prevalent practice is the use of holy water which one may drink, pour over the body or apply to an ailing part of the body. Through these means, God often brings healing to those who pray for it.[51] This water conveys the healing energies of God by virtue of the Holy Spirit, whom the priest asks Christ to send down during the ritual blessing of the waters, especially during the feast of Theophany. After having prayed "for the sanctification of this water through the power, operation and presence of the Holy Spirit," and "for the descent upon these waters of the purifying action of the Holy Spirit," the priest asks God to "change this water into a gift of sanctification . . . for the healing of soul and body," and to make it "a fountain of incorruption . . . the healing of the sick, the crushing of demons," and again "that it may remain inaccessible to the powers of the enemy, filled with the power of angels and that, in drawing and tasting it, all might use it effectively for the purification of their souls and bodies." The celebrant then adds the following prayer: "Give to all those who touch it, are anointed with it and taste of it, sanctification, purification and health."[52]

God's healing grace may also be effected through the laying on of hands, according to Christ's promise: "those who believe . . . will lay their hands on the sick, and they will recover" (Mk 16:18), and according to his own example given on numerous occasions.[53] Together

---

[50]Cf., e.g., Callinicos, *Life of Hypatios* IV.7; IX.6; XII.10; XV.2. Palladius, *Lausiac History* XII.1; XVIII.11, 22. *History of the Monks of Egypt* I.12, 16; IX.11; XXI.17. *Life of St Theodore of Sykeon* 68, 85, 107, 112, 145, 154, 156.

[51]See, among others, St John Cassian, *Conferences* XV.4. Theodoret of Cyrus, *History of the monks of Syria* XXXVI.14. St Barsanuphius, *Letters* 643. *Life of St Theodore of Sykeon* 31, 83, 97, 106, 111, 145.

[52]The complete text of the rite may be found in Mercenier, *op. cit.*, t. II-1, 273-285.

[53]Cf. Mt 9:18; 19:13-15; Mk 5:23; 6:5; 7:32; 8:23-25; 10:16; Lk 4:40; 13;13.

with this act through which the power of the Holy Spirit is conveyed is found the *epiklesis*,[54] the prayer asking Christ to send the Spirit in the Father's name.[55]

The Sign of the Cross

The sign of the cross is also a traditional means of healing. Beyond the fact that it too invokes and effects the energies of the Holy Trinity, it is the effective sign of Christ's victory over death and corruption, over sin and the power of the devil and of demons, and consequently over the illness connected with them. The healing power of the cross is clearly expressed by the Orthodox Church in the services of the Exaltation of the Holy Cross (Sept. 14). They refer to the cross repeatedly as the "physician of the sick" and evoke the Old Testament prefiguration of the bronze serpent that Moses raised on a staff, which became a remedy for those who had been bitten by serpents (Num 21:6-9).[56]

Exorcism: Its Role and Meaning

Finally we must mention exorcism, which holds a unique and important place among the religious healing arts.

According to the Church Fathers, the devil and demons are at the root of certain illnesses. Most often their activity is manifested indirectly, but in certain instances it takes the form of possession.

---

[54]Cf., for example, Acts 28:8.

[55]Examples of such healings may be found in Acts 9:17; 28:8. Callinicos, *Life of Hypatios* XXV.1. Theodoret, *op. cit.*, IX.7. Palladius, *Lausiac History* XII.1; XVIII.21. *Life of St Theodore of Sykeon* 69.154. Cf. St Irenaeus, *Adv. Haer.* II.32.4. On this subject, see also Harnack, *op. cit.*, 66.

[56]Many cases of healing by means of the sign of the cross are cited by F.J. Dölger, "Beiträge zur Geschichte des Kreuzzeichens," VII.16: "Das Kreuzzeichen in der Volksmedizin," *Jahrbuch für Antike und Chirstentum*, 7, 1964, 5-16. See especially, Callinicos, *op. cit.*, IV.8; XXII.9, 14. St Gregory of Nyssa, *Life of St Macrina* 31. Theodoret, *op. cit.*, IX.7; XXII.4, 5. St John Moschus, *The Spiritual Meadow* 56. *Miracles of Saints Cosmas and Damian* 28, ed. Deubner, 171-172. *Life of St Theodore of Sykeon* 31, 65, 67, 68, 72, 83, 85, 95, 110, 113.

A demon—or possibly several—may enter the body and the soul of a person and make its abode there, ravaging and ruining the person's health,[57] "inflicting sickness and serious accidents upon the body, and on the soul, unforeseen and extraordinary troubles through the use of violence."[58] The evangelists,[59] the Fathers and the authors of the *Lives* of saints recount many such cases.

Many of our contemporaries are tempted to view references to possession as an archaic understanding of phenomena that modern medicine is now able to explain scientifically and can quite easily assimilate into its analyses of the mind. However, the experience of spiritual elders—and even a simple reading of scriptural texts and hagiographies—belies such a vision of reality and reveals one that is far more complex. Thus, if we refer to the Gospels, we observe that possession and illness, or infirmities, are presented as orders of reality situated on two different planes, each with its own attributes, and not necessarily connected to one another. First of all, possession and illness, or infirmities, are clearly distinguished in a number of passages.[60] This fact alone makes it impossible to equate the two. Secondly, the majority of illnesses, or infirmities, referred to in connection with the miracles of Christ are not shown to be in any way connected with possession. Thirdly, in certain cases, a person may be afflicted with both possession and illness (or infirmity) without the two conditions having any correlation. Thus St Matthew says: ". . . they brought to him many who were possessed with demons; and he cast out the spirits with a word, and healed all who were sick" (8:16). We see here that Christ undertakes two consecutive actions: one is an exorcism, the other a healing. However, the first action would have sufficed had the illness and the possession been one and the same, or

---

[57]Cf. Tertullien, *Apologia* XXXVII.9.

[58]Ibid., XXII.4. Cf. Tatian, *Discourse with the Greeks* 18.

[59]Cf. O Böcher, Chirstus Exorcista, *Dämonismus und Taufe im Neuen Testament* (Stuttgart, 1972).

[60]Cf. Mt 4:24; 8:16; 10:1, 8; Mk 1:32, 34; 3:2, 10-11; 6:13; 16:17-18. Lk 4:40; 6:18; 7:21; 8:2; 9:1; 13:32. Naturally, the Fathers make the same distinction. For Theodoret, see A. Adnès and P. Canivet, "Guérisons miraculeuses et exorcismes dans l'histoire: Philothée de Theodoret de Cyr," *Revue de l'Histoire des Religions*, 171, 1967, 166-174.

had the one been caused by the other. These various arguments lead to the conclusion that illness is to be regarded as independent, with its own etiology. Nor is this the case only for a certain category of illness or infirmity: those that are considered in some instances to be the result of possession are the same as those that in other cases are regarded implicitly as having natural causes. This is why we see in the Gospels deaf, dumb or blind men who are not considered to be possessed,[61] while others who exhibit the same symptoms are regarded as such.[62] Likewise, some paralytics owe their condition to possession,[63] others do not.[64] The same distinction holds true for those suffering from epilepsy: some are said to be possessed,[65] while others are clearly differentiated from the "demoniacs."[66] It is evident, therefore, that the assertion of a demoniac etiology is in no way due to an inability to explain the condition in any other way, and shows that natural causes are not the only causes. Furthermore, it is not the symptoms of a particular illness or infirmity that serve to identify whether it is of natural or demonic origin since, in both cases, they often appear quite similar. Only a spiritual sight, gifted with the charism of discernment (cf. 1 Cor 12:10), is able to make the distinction.

Through these various considerations, we begin to perceive the complexity of this reality and the differences that exist between the clinical perspective of medical science, which makes judgments solely on the level of phenomena — from material appearances — and

---

[61]Cf. Mt 9:27-30; 15:30-31; 20:29-34 [// Mk 10:49-53 // Lk 18:35-43]. Mk 7:32-35; 8:22-25 [// Jn 9:17]; 10:46-53.

[62]Cf. Mt 9:32-33 [Lk 11:14]; 12:22; 9:17-27. The same distinction can be seen, for example, in the *Life of St Theodore of Sykeon*: 94 (dumb demoniac); 61, 65, 67, 95, 110 (dumb, non-possessed).

[63]Cf. Lk 13:10-16.

[64]Cf. Mt 4:24; 9:2-7 // Mk 2:3-12 // Lk 5:18, 25. The same distinction is made, for example, in Callinicos, *Life of Hypatios* IX.4-6 for the first instance; XXXVI.6 for the second.

[65]Cf. Mt 17:14-18 // Mk 9:17-22 // Lk 9:38-42, and in the *Life of St Theodore of Sykeon* 108 and 156 for the first instance; 68, 83, 85, 102, 107, 110, 154, 156, 159 for the second.

[66]Cf. Mt 4:24.

spiritual perception which goes to the very essence of things, adding to the "science" of appearances the knowledge of their fundamental reality.

Thus, if one recognizes demonic possession in a given illness or infirmity, which in another instance may have purely natural causes, one may choose to resort to an exorcism.

Christ's casting out of demons is one of the signs of salvation: ". . . if it is by the Spirit of God that I cast out demons, then the kingdom of God has come upon you" (Mt 12:28). And St John says: "The reason the Son of God appeared was to destroy the works of the devil" (1 Jn 3:8). Through the sin of Adam, the power of the devil and of demons was loosed and spread over the whole world to perform wicked deeds within it. Through the work of Christ, the New Adam, this power was broken and subjected once again to the power of the Spirit. Mankind is reunited with God in the Person of the incarnate Word and recovers the blessedness of his original state and his original destiny. This is what Christ has shown in conferring upon the twelve Apostles, then on the seventy-two disciples, power and authority over the demons, to cast them out (Lk 9:1; Mt 10:1; Mk 3:15), as well as to trample under foot the "power of the enemy." Solely through the invocation of the Name of Christ, Satan's kingdom is brought to ruin as he falls from the sky like lightning (cf. Lk 10:17-18), and the nations "turn from darkness to light, from the power of Satan to God" (Acts 26:18). Through baptism, Satan's power of subjection over man is reduced to a power of suggestion, while every Christian is given the ability to resist and to make him flee (Jas 4:7).[67] To some is given, as it was given to the Apostles, the power to cast demons out of those whom they possess, and thus to heal the illness which may be caused by this possession.

The charism of exorcism was widespread in early Christianity, and many authors refer to it as if it were a common practice.[68]

---

[67]Cf. St Cyprian of Carthage, *a Donat* V.

[68]Cf. Origen, *Adv. Celsus* I.46. St Theophilus of Antioch, *To Autolycus* II.8. St Cyprian of Carthage, *a Demetrianus* 15; *Quod idola dii non sint* 7. Lactantius, *Divinae Institutiones* IV.27.

According to Origen, "there remain among Christians traces of this Spirit that appeared in the form of a dove; they cast out demons and healed many illnesses."[69] And according to St Justin, "there are in our world and in our city many demoniacs who have been cured neither by exorcism, nor by enchantments, nor by potions. Our Christians, through imprecations in the Name of Jesus Christ who was crucified under Pontius Pilate, have healed and, to this day, continue to heal many of them by subduing and casting out the demons which possess them."[70]

Exorcism is a sign that Christ has come to restore to mankind the kingdom which we had lost and to reclaim on our behalf the power we had given up to Satan. It has its place under the Name of the Lord of hosts.[71] It is in the Name of Christ that demons are subdued and cast out.[72] As Tertullian said: "all the sway and the power we hold over them draws its strength from our pronouncing the name of Christ."[73] And according to St Justin, "every demon exorcised in the Name of this Son of God . . . is vanquished and subdued."[74] Furthermore, they cannot bear to hear this Name:[75] they fear it above all else because it signifies their defeat and their punishment.[76]

The invocation of the Name of Christ, while necessary, may nevertheless be insufficient for this work: God conveys his victorious strength to a person only if he is worthy to receive it. To those who invoke his Name, he grants this power only in proportion to their faith and to the purity of their hearts. We may recall the passage in

---

[69] *Adv. Celsus* I.46.

[70] *Second Apology* 6.

[71] In his *Dialogue* (30), Justin takes this traditional Old Testament reference and associates it with the victory over demons.

[72] Cf. Lk 9:49-50; 10:17. Mk 9:38. St Irenaeus, *Adv. Haer.* II.6,2. Origen, *Adv. Celsus* I.6; III.24. Theodoret, *History of the Monks of Syria* XXII. The sign of the cross is also used, the seal of Christ, the mark of his victory over death. Cf. Athanasius, *Life of Antony* XXXV; *On the Incarnation* XLVII.2. Callinicos, *Life of Hypatios* XXII.14.

[73] *Apologia* XXIII.15. Cf. Origen, *Adv. Celsus* I.6.

[74] *Dialogue* 85.

[75] Cf. Athanasius, *Life of Antony* XL; XLI.

[76] St Justin, *Dialogue* 30. Tertullian, *Apologia* XXIII, 15-16. Origen, *Adv. Celsus* I.6.

the Gospels where the disciples were said to be unable to free an epileptic man from the demon that held him. After Christ had cast out this demon, his disciples asked: "Why could we not cast it out?" Christ's answer: "Because of your little faith" (Mt 17:19, 20). It is so that we might understand the necessity of an unflinching faith and an unwavering dedication to Christ that he says again: ". . . no one who does a mighty work in my name will be able soon after to speak evil of me" (Mk 9:39). "Abba Pytirion, the disciple of Abba Antony, once said: 'he who wishes to cast out demons must first subdue passion [within himself].' "[77] If a person wishing to perform an exorcism has not united himself sufficiently to Christ through purification of the passions and the practice of virtue, the power of the demons may turn against him. The account of the Jewish exorcist in the Book of Acts (19:13-17) attests to this fact. They "undertook to pronounce the name of the Lord Jesus over those who had evil spirits, saying, 'I adjure you by the Jesus whom Paul preaches' . . . But the evil spirits answered them, 'Jesus I know, and Paul I know; but who are you?' And the man in whom the evil spirit was leaped in them, mastered all of them, and overpowered them, so that they fled out of that house naked and wounded." It is through the holiness of their lives that St Paul, the other Apostles and the saints give strength to their invocation of the Name of Jesus; it is only in this way that his power can be poured out. Apart from purity, humility is the one virtue the exorcist must possess, for without it he can do nothing:[78] for only when a man has recognized his own impotence and cast off his own self is Christ able to dwell within him and clothe him with divine power in the name of the Father and through the Spirit. Finally, the exorcist must be moved by a profound love for his neighbor and act purely out of compassion rather than for a specific end.

Though it may appear to be so at first glance, exorcism is not a technique; it does not work like some magical process through a

---

[77] *Apophthegmata*, Pytirion, 1.

[78] St Athanasius, *Life of Antony* XXXVIII. The *Lives* of saints reveal that it is the "simple ones" who have the greatest power over demons. See, for example, Palladius, *Lausiac History* XXII, "Paul the Simple," par. 9, and XLIV, "Life of St Innocent."

particular spell. Its effectiveness depends above all on the spiritual well-being of the one putting it into practice. As Harnack emphasizes, "it is not the prayer that heals, but the one who prays; it is not the formula but the Spirit; it is not the exorcism but the exorcist."[79]

Although exorcisms were prevalent in the age of nascent Christianity, along with miraculous healings, they became far less frequent in subsequent centuries. Some of the reasons for this have already been stated insofar as exorcisms also possess, in addition to their immediate purpose, a certain value as "signs." Nevertheless, especially with the expansion of Christianity, demonic activity, while maintaining its intensity, has changed shape and begun to manifest itself differently: it has become diluted, more subtle, harder to pinpoint and less overt. St John Cassian wrote: "We can see, both through our experience and through the witness of the elders, that demons in our age no longer have the power they once had." And he offers two possible explanations for this phenomenon: "either the virtue of the Cross, which has penetrated to the deepest desert, and the grace of the Cross, which shines in every place, have suppressed the malice of demons; or else . . . the end of their visible attacks has served to deceive us and to inflict upon us yet crueler defeats."[80] According to this second explanation, demons direct their attacks especially against those who lead spiritual lives and, to escape their vigilance, take on forms and use means that make them less susceptible to spiritual discernment.

While they ceased quite early on to be a common recourse for healing, exorcisms are nevertheless still practiced in certain cases and have proved to be effective in freeing many from their illnesses or infirmities.[81]

---

[79] *Op. cit.*, 106.

[80] *Conferences* VII.23.

[81] Many cases are recounted in the *Life of St Theodore of Sykeon*. On the practice of exorcisms in present-day Russia, see the testimony of T. Gorichéva, *Parler de Dieu est dangereux* (Paris, 1985), 137-139.

The Role of Secular Medicine

Along with all these specifically religious means of healing, Christians have had recourse, since the beginning of the Christian era and in direct continuity with Old Testament tradition, to any secular means of healing that the medical science of their age has had to offer.

We know that the evangelist Luke was a physician by trade;[82] however, we are not told whether he continued to practice this art after his conversion. Nevertheless, ever since the first centuries, many Christians are known to have worked as physicians. Eusebius of Caesarea refers specifically to Alexander the Phrygian, "a physician by trade, practicing in the region of Gaul, and known to all for his love of God."[83] Many of them were priests, such as Zenobius, priest and physician of Sidon,[84] and Peter, "adorned with the honor of the priesthood, but also with the art that heals the body."[85] Some were even bishops, such as Tiberias;[86] Basil of Ancyra, who lived under Constantine and of whom Jerome said that he had become "knowledgeable in the medical arts";[87] Theodoret, the physician, bishop of Laodicea, of whom Eusebius writes that "even through his works this man fulfilled his given name[88] and the role of bishop, and he was successful above all in the science of healing the body";[89] John, the bishop of Trimithontos, in Cyprus.[90] Or again, Gerantios, a Greek physician who was consecrated bishop of Nicomedia and gained great popularity by continuing to practice his art among the people.[91]

---

[82]Col 4:14.

[83]*Ecclesiastical History* V.1.49. Cf. Harnack, *op. cit.*, 40-41.

[84]Eusebius, *op. cit.*, VIII.13. Harnack, *op. cit.*, 44-45.

[85]Theodoret of Cyrus, *Letters* 114.

[86]Cf. Harnack, *op. cit.*, 45-46.

[87]*Des hommes illustres* 89.

[88]*Theodoret* refers here to a kind of remedy.

[89]Eusebius, *op. cit.*, VII.32; cf. 23. Cf. Harnack, *op. cit.*, 45.

[90]Theodoret of Paphos, *La Légende de St Spyridon, évêque de Trimithonte*, Louvain, 1953, 15-16, 91-92.

[91]Sozomen, *Ecclesiastical History* VIII.6.3-9.

In Syria, Patriarch Theodosius was a famous physician,[92] and Politianos continued to practice his art on occasion after his election as patriarch of Alexandria.[93] We could cite many other examples.[94] We also know the interest of several Church Fathers and the esteem in which they held the medical arts. Among them were Gregory of Nyssa,[95] St Gregory of Nazianzus and St Basil who began to learn medicine in the course of their studies,[96] Nemesius, bishop of Emessa,[97] St Isidore of Pelusia,[98] St Theodore of Sykeon,[99] St Photius, the Patriarch,[100] and Meletios the Monk.[101]

Furthermore, we know that in Rome, around the year 200, Christians began to read and appreciate the works of Galen.[102] This interest in Galen's medicine grew and spread to such an extent that by the third century his diagnostic and therapeutic methods had come to influence the whole of the Christian world.[103] When they refer to physiology or bodily medicine, the Fathers commonly use the categories established by Hyppocrates and Galen,[104] which were adopted

[92]According to Barhebraeus' *Chronique syriaque.* Cf. R. Duval, *La littérature syriaque* (Paris, 1899), 273.

[93]Cf. Papadopoulos, *Historia tès Ekklèsias Alexandrias* (Alexandria, 1935), 511-512.

[94]Cf. Harnack, *op. cit.*, chap. 1, "Christliche Ärzte," 37-50. D.J. Constantellos, "Physician priests in the Medieval Greek Church," *The Greek Orthodox Theological Review*, 12, 1966-1967, 141-153.

[95]See M.E. Keenan, "St Gregory of Nyssa and the Medical Profession," *Bulletin of the History of Medicine*, 15, 1944, 150-161.

[96]Cf. St Gregory of Nazianzus, *Eulogy of St Basil*, XXIII.6. See M.E. Keenan, "St Gregory of Nazianzus and Early Byzantine Medicine," *Bulletin of the History of Medicine*, 9, 1941, 8-30. M.M. Fox, *The Life and Times of St Basil the Great as Revealed in His Works*, "Catholic University Patristic Series" no. 57 (Washington, 1939), 13-17.

[97]See his famous treatise, *On the Nature of Man*, PG 40.504-818.

[98]Cf. *Letters* 71, 191, 228.

[99]Cf. P. Hordern, "Saints and Doctors in the Early Byzantine Empire, the Case of Theodore of Sykeon," *Studies in Church History*, 19, 1982, 1-13.

[100]Cf. *Letters* 230, ed. J. Valetta, London, 1864, 543-544. W. Treadgolg, *The Nature of the Bibliotheca of Photius* (Washington, 1980), 103.

[101]See his treatise: *On the Making of Man*, PG 64.1075-1310.

[102]Cf. Harnack, *op. cit.*, 42.

[103]P. Lain Entralgo, *op. cit.*, 93, 94.

[104]Cf., among others, Basil of Ancyra, *De Virginitate* IX; XII. St Gregory of Nyssa, *Treatise on Virginity* XXII.1-2; *The Creation of Man* I, XII, XIII, XXX; *Homilies on the Our Father* IV.2. St Basil of Caesarea, *Hexameron* V.4, 5, 8. St Symeon

by Byzantine medicine[105] that was founded upon them, yet nevertheless developed in new ways.[106] Given the structure of Byzantine
society, such a development in medical research and its application
would necessarily have been endorsed by Church authorities,[107] especially since in the Byzantine Empire, monasteries and ecclesiastical
schools seem to have been the main centers of medical education.[108]

Medicine is generally seen as a very special way of putting charity into practice.[109] Nevertheless, at other times the misuse of the
medical arts is denounced along with the misdeeds of certain physicians.[110] We conclude that the art of healing the body falls to the

---

the New Theologian, *Catechesis* XXV.65-68. Theodoret of Cyrus, *History of the
Monks of Syria* XVII.5, 8; *Thérapeutique des maladies helléniques* V.82; *Discourse on
Providence* III, IV, VI. About this author, on this subject, see P. Canivet, *Histoire d'une
entreprise apologétique au Vè siècle* (Paris, 1958), 117 and 307-308; "Guérisons mirac-
uleuses et exorcismes dans l'Histoire: Philothée de Théodoret de Cyr," 71-75; *Le
Monachisme Syrien selon Théodoret de Cyr* (Paris, 1977), 132.

[105]The great Byzantine physicians, Oribase (4th c.), Jacques le Psychestre (5th
c.), Caelius Aurelianus (5th c.), Aetius of Amida (6th c.), Alexander of Tralles (6th-
7th c.), Paul of Egina (7th c.), Theophilus Protospatharios (7th c.), Theophanes Nan-
nos (10th c.) and Michael Psellos (11th c.) are known as encyclopedists and compilers
of the ruling Galen tradition. Cf. Brunet, "Les médecins grecs depuis la mort de
Galien jusqu'à la fin de l'Empire d'Orient," in Laignel-Lavastine, *Histoire générale de
la médecine* (Paris, 1936), t. I, 433-463.

[106]The original contributions of Byzantine medicine have recently been emphasized from several perspectives. See the various contributions compiled by J. Scar-
borough, *Symposium on Byzantine Medicine, Dumbarton Oaks Papers*, 38 (Washington,
1985).

[107]Cf. S.S. Harakas, "'Rational Medicine' in the Orthodox Tradition," *The Greek
Orthodox Theological Review*, 33, 1988, 24-30.

[108]O. Temkin, "Byzantine Medicine, Tradition and Empiricism," *Dumbarton
Oaks Papers*, 16, 1962, 111.

[109]Cf. St Basil: "All of you who practice medicine are also called to be philan-
thropists" (*Letters* CLXXXIX.1). See T.S. Miller, *The Birth of the Hospital in the
Byzantine Empire* (Baltimore, 1985), 50-62.

[110]These criticisms are common in the *Lives* of the saints. See T.S. Miller, *op. cit.*,
62-66; P. Hordern, *op. cit.*, 1-13; V. Nutton, "From Galen to Alexander, Aspects of
Medicine in Medieval Practice in Late Antiquity," in *Symposium on Byzantine Medicine, Dumbarton Oaks Papers*, 38, 1985, 6; H.J. Magoulias, "The Lives of Saints as
Sources of Data for the History of Byzantine Medicine in the Sixth and Seventh
Centuries," *Byzantinische Zeitschrift*, 57, 1964, 129-132; A. Kazhdan, "The Image of
the Medical Doctor in Byzantine Literature of the Tenth to Twelfth Centuries," in

good and the evil alike,[111] and that, from a spiritual perspective, the value of medicine lies in the orientation of the one who implements it.[112] The Fathers consider that physicians practice a profession like any other—aligning himself with current classifications, St Basil lists them among the artisans—and that their professional education, therefore, is not meant to be any more spiritual than that of a carpenter or a ship's captain and ought to take place in existing schools.[113] With regard to the treatment of physical illness, the Church does not profess any doctrines strictly its own,[114] but rather accepts the current diagnostic and therapeutic methods of the society in which it exists.[115] As St Gregory Palamas affirms: in the area of physiology, there is freedom of opinion.[116]

Nothing, therefore, stands in the way of Christians in need calling on physicians and following their prescriptions, according to the advice of Sirach: "And give the physician his place, for the Lord created him; do not let him leave you, for there is need of him. There is a time when success lies in the hands of physicians" (38:12-13). When the opportunity arises, the Fathers make the same recommendation.

Symposium on Byzantine Medicine, Dumbarton Oaks Papers, 38, 1985, 43-51, passim. Note the expression used by St Mark (5:26) as he recounts the story of the woman with the flow of blood: ". . . a woman who had had a flow of blood for twelve years, and *who had suffered much under many physicians . . .*"

[111]Cf. Origen, *Adv. Celsus* III.12; VI.96.

[112]Cf. Origen, ibid., III.13; *Homilies on Numbers* XVIII.3.

[113]Cf. Origen, *Adv. Celsus* III.13.

[114]The condemnation of a group of Christians who were attending the school of Galen, in Rome around the year 200 (cf. Eusebius, *Ecclesiastical History* V, XXVIII.14-15), seems to be due not so much to their subscription to the medical notions of this school as to the philosophical theories it promoted along with them (cf. Harnack, *op. cit.,* 40-41). The famous unmercenary physicians, Sts Cosmas and Damien, and St Pantaleimon are presented through their hagiographies as having been formed in the medical tradition of Hypocrates and Galen (cf. "Vita SS Cosmae et Damiani," *Analecta Bollandiana,* I, 1882, 589. Symeon Metaphrastes, *Life of St Pantaleimon,* PG 115.448-449).

[115]See T.S. Miller, *op. cit.,* 163-166. M.E. Keenan, "St Gregory of Nazianzus and Early Byzantine Medicine," 26-30; "St Gregory of Nyssa and the Medical Profession," 154-157.

[116]*Triads* II.2.30.

Origen affirms that "medicine is useful and necessary to mankind."[117]
"In time of illness, nothing stands in the way of calling for physicians," notes Diadochus of Photike.[118] St Barsanuphius writes that
"we are well aware that those who are ill have need of a physician and
of his cures."[119] According to St Basil, "it is mere obstinacy to refuse
help from the art of physicians."[120] St Theodoret of Cyrus notes the
practice current in his time: "It is customary for those who suffer the
assaults of sickness to call upon physicians and to make the weapons
of science their allies against every illness."[121]

Furthermore, it is under the influence of certain Christians that
medicine has become a social institution. Fr Stanley Harakas writes
that "it is the Orthodox Church that took the initiative to organize
the medical profession into the systematic treatment and care of
patients in a hospital setting. Not only did Church men speak highly
of physicians, but they made use of them in ways unknown until then
to fulfill the philanthropic goals of the Church. The Byzantine hospital is the most conclusive proof of a sane and salutary synergy
between the Orthodox Christian tradition and rational medicine."[122]
We may assume, in fact, that it was in Byzantium, in the fourth century, that the precursors of modern hospitals came about, and that the
Church herself had taken the initiative in hiring, paying and organ-
izing the services of professional physicians.[123] T.S. Miller does not
hesitate to write that "the Byzantine *xenones* represent not only the
first public institutions to offer medical services to the sick, but also
the main current in the development of hospitals throughout the
Middle Ages, and out of which the Latin West and the Muslim East
were equally inspired for their own medical structures. Retracing the
advent and development of medical centers for the sick within the
Byzantine Empire amounts to writing the first chapter of the history

---

[117] *Adv. Celsus* III.12.
[118] *One Hundred Chapters* 53.
[119] *Letters* 424.
[120] *Great Rules* 55.
[121] *Discourse on Providence* III.
[122] "'Rational Medicine' in the Orthodox Tradition," 31.
[123] See T.S. Miller, *op. cit.*, 4.

of hospitals themselves."[124] Two Church Fathers played an especially important role in this process: St Basil and St John Chrysostom. The first had a hospital built in 370, in a suburb of Caesarea, with all the necessary qualified staff.[125] This foundation, referred to as a "basiliade," after his name, became the model for many others in Cappadocia and in other provinces.[126] St John Chrysostom opened several hospitals in Constantinople at the beginning of the fifth century.[127] These two are not isolated examples. The Church of Alexandria, at the bishop's behest, created a corps of nurses who, in the years 416 to 418, numbered more than five hundred.[128] When Theodoret became bishop of Cyrus, he sought to create a corps of physicians,[129] and possibly even to found a clinic.[130] Theodore of Petra recounts that St Theodosius built, within the walls of his monastery, "a house where [the monks] could conveniently be healed of their bodily illnesses, and also designated another house for the people of the world who might have need of medical attention; likewise, finally, for any of the beggars who might be sick he had built a separate, special hospital." At the same time he created a "corps of various officers" to "effect the healing of the sick through treatment" which he himself would prescribe for the illness "in accordance with each case."[131] Another famous monastic hospital in the twelfth century was that of the Monastery of the Pantocrator, whose typikon[132] reveals a highly professional organization, with medical treatment carried out by

---

[124]Ibid. The medical historian, H. Sigerist, is of the same opinion ("An Outline of the Development of the Hospital," *Bulletin of the History of Medicine*, 4, 1936, 579.

[125]Cf. Gregory of Nazianzus, *Eulogy of Basil* LXIII, 1. *Letters* XCIV, ed. Courtonne, vol. I, 206. See T.S. Miller, *op. cit.*, 86-87.

[126]Bihlmeyer-Tuchle, *Histoire de l'Eglise*, t. I (Paris, 1969), 343.

[127]Palladius, *Dialogue on the Life of John Chrysostom* V, SC 341, 122.

[128]Ibid.

[129]Theodoret of Cyrus, *Letters* 114, 115.

[130]Cf. P. Canivet, Introduction à Théodoret, *Thérapeutique des maladies helléniques*, SC 57, t. I (Paris, 1958), 18-19, 47.

[131]*Life of St Theodosius* 16.

[132]The typikon is the "rule" according to which the organization and functions within a monastery are established.

well-equipped, specialized teams, precisely ordered and made up of physicians and medical aides. This hospital comprised five specialized clinics and disposed of every necessity to fulfill its tasks.[133] These cases are not exceptional: most monastic communities (monasteries, sketes ...) had their own infirmaries and attendants,[134] and even their own physicians who were sometimes monks.[135] The state hospitals themselves were partly staffed with clerics, many of whom were appointed as their directors.[136] The considerable participation of monks and clergy in the advent and operation of medical establishments, both within and outside of monastic settings, would certainly not have been possible without the support of ecclesiastical authorities. This support remained overt up to the last days of the Byzantine Empire,[137] but also under the Turkish occupation,[138] and was eventually continued in Russia in the following centuries.[139]

---

[133]All the details concerning equipment, administration, personnel, treatments and the social origin of the patients can be found in "Le Typikon du Christ Sauveur Pantocrator," ed. P. Gautier, *Revue des Etudes Byzantines*, 32, 1974, 1-145, and in the excellent summary of T.S. Miller, *op. cit.*, 12-21.

[134]Cf., for example, *Life of St Dosithée* I.4. *Life of St Athanasius the Athonite* 37.

[135]Cf. *Apophthegmata* 1493. Cyril of Scythopolis, *Life of St Sabas* 131, 26. In his *Lausiac History* VII.4, Palladius notes that some physicians lived on the mountain near the desert of Nitria. In chap. XIII.1 and 2, he adds that in the same area there was an Appolonius who served in a certain measure as a pharmacist, "buying all sorts of medical products and provisions in Alexandria which he then distributed to the sick brethren of the community." On the organization of hospital care in Byzantium in the 6th and 7th centuries, see H.J. Magoulias, *art. cit.*, 133-138. For the whole of the Byzantine period, see T.S. Miller, *The Birth of the Hospital in the Byzantine Empire* (Baltimore, 1985), "Byzantine Hospitals," in *Symposium on Byzantine Medicine, Dumbarton Oaks Papers*, 38, 1985, 53-63.

[136]Cf. D.J. Constantellos, "Physician-Priests in the Medieval Greek Church," 146-148. T.S. Miller, "Byzantine Hospitals," 59.

[137]T.S. Miller, *The Birth of the Hospital in the Byzantine Empire* (Baltimore, 1985), 33-34.

[138]See S.S. Harakas, "The Eastern Orthodox Tradition," in *Caring and Curing, Health and Medicine in the Western Religious Tradition*, R.L. Numbers and D.W. Amundsen, eds., New York, 1986, 161-164.

[139]See F. Dorbeck, "Origin of Medicine in Russia," *Medical Life*, 3, 1923, 223-233. N. Mandelker Frieden, *Russian Physicians in an Era of Reform and Revolution, 1865-1905* (Princeton, 1981).

Thus, in practice, whether in ecclesiastical and monastic settings or in the "world," resorting to secular medicine does not appear to pose any problems.[140]

MAXIMALIST POSITIONS

Such recourse may nevertheless be surprising after all that has been said concerning the spiritual definition that Christianity has given to the first cause of illness, concerning its own ability to offer a means of healing the whole human being, concerning its establishment, therefore, of specifically religious methods of healing, especially insofar as it considers Christ to be the only physician.

There are Christians who, particularly in light of this last principle, refuse to resort to secular medicine when they are ill.

Tatian and Tertullian go so far as to condemn such recourse, considering the use of medicine to be illegitimate: "Let us leave theses means to the pagans! Our bulwark is faith," affirms Tertullian.[141] And Tatian writes that "any healing through remedies is a delusion, for if one is healed through his trust in the properties of matter, he will be so the more by giving himself over to the power of God. Why would a person who puts his trust in matter not put his trust in God?"[142] Arnobius of Sicca likewise attacks medicine which he considers to be a manifestation of pagan culture, accusing it of being founded on human knowledge rather than on the power of God which is effective without recourse to herbs or ointments.[143]

Such stances on principle are nevertheless quite rare. In each of these three cases, they arise from a dubious rigorism, linked in the

---

[140]What was true in Antiquity and in the Middle Ages remains so to this day. This has been demonstrated by research of S.S. Harakas, whose findings are summed up in his article: "'Rational Medicine' in Orthodox Tradition," 40-43. See also his work, "The Eastern Orthodox Tradition," 165-167.

[141]*Scorpiaces* I.

[142]*Discourse with the Greeks* 20.

[143]*Adversus gentes* I.48, PL 5.779B-781A; III.23, 969A.

first instance to Montanism,[144] in the second to Encratism,[145] while the third is presumably influenced by the marcionites.[146] Therefore they cannot be considered normative for Christianity as a whole.[147]

This said, certain monastic settings have made it a practice to forego secular medicine. Thus St Gregory Palamas notes that "some spiritual Fathers do not allow the monks to take baths for reasons of health,[148] nor to resort to medical care when they are ill, because they are wholly committed to God, they depend on him completely, and because God undoubtedly fulfills all their needs for their own good."[149] St Barsanuphius is also known to have counseled often against the use of physicians and of medicine. To one of his spiritual children who asked him whether he should resort to remedies in the event of an illness he said: "Place all your hope in your Master and you will find comfort."[150] To another he said: "Those who in their illness have come to scorn medicine . . . have reached the highest degree of faith."[151] A third wrote to him saying: "My thoughts tell me: 'when you are struck with physical illness, you should show it to a physician, because you are not capable of being healed without medicine.' But

---

[144]The *Scorpiaces*, from which Tertullian is cited, very likely dates back to the year 213, while it is generally agreed that his separation from the Church and his adherence to the Montanist movement took place in 207.

[145]Tatian's *Discourse with the Greeks*, from which this citation is taken, is a passionately polemical work that condemns unilaterally and without any kind of discernment all that belongs to Greek culture. Furthermore, it dates back to Tatian's separation from the Church and his founding of the Encratite movement.

[146]Cf. F. Schweidweiler, "Arnobius und der Marcionitismus," *Zeitschrift für neutestamentliche Wissenschaft und die Kunde der älteren Kirche*, 45, 1954, 42-67. Marcion was extremely hostile toward medicine. See H. Schadewaldt, "Die Apologie der Heilkunst bei den Kirchenvätern," *Veröffentlichungen der internationalen Gesellschaft Für Geschichte der Pharmazie*, 26, 1965, 127.

[147]See D.W. Amundsen, "Medicine and Faith in Early Christianity," *Bulletin of the History of Medicine*, 56, 1982, 343-350.

[148]Bath-therapy was one of the main forms of treatment recommended by hyppocratic-galenic medicine. This method of healing is cited, for example, by Theodoret, *Discours sur la Providence* II.581B, and by St Gregory of Nazianzus, *Oration XXVIII*, 61-64.

[149]*Triads* II.1.35.

[150]*Letters* 32.

[151]*Letters* 529.

then they say: 'Do not resort to these remedies, but rather to the holiness of the saints, and let that alone suffice.' I pray you, compassionate Father, tell me which of these thoughts I must heed." St Barsanuphius answered: "Brother, when I see you worry about physical illness, I think that the Fathers do not share this preoccupation. The second thought, therefore, is better than the first."[152] He goes on to demonstrate this by comparing the two positions at length. The first thought, he notes, conveys a lack of faith, a certain "timidity, akin to the pusillanimity that is the root of a weak faith, the mother of doubt which separates one from God." It leads one to doubt Providence, it takes the heart captive and subjects it to evil preoccupations, it leads to a lack of vigilance, to a troubled and despondent soul. The second thought, on the other hand, manifests "a perfect faith in God," "it implies a patience that leads to a test of virtue (Rom 5:4) from which hope is born," it leads to trust in God, removes captivity and "frees man from his cares that he might cast all his burdens on the Lord." It leads one to believe that "He who sees every hidden illness is also able to heal my illness," it brings peace to one's soul, keeping it from *accedia*, it leads one to thanksgiving and helps man to bear his illness through his participation in the endurance of Job.[153] From this same perspective St Macarius wrote: "Do not bodily illnesses lead you at times to consult earthly physicians, as if Christ, to whom you entrusted yourself, were unable to heal you? See how you deceive yourself, because you imagine that you have faith while you do not truly believe, though you ought to. If you believed that Christ heals the eternal and incurable wounds of your immortal soul and its every illness caused by vices, you would also believe that he is able to heal the transitory pains and sickness of your body, and you would rely on Him alone, ignoring the resources and cares of physicians."[154]

St Barsanuphius recognizes, however, that this is an ideal to which few can attain and which therefore must not be imposed on others.[155] St Gregory Palamas likewise justified it on the basis of the

---

[152]*Letters* 532.
[153]Ibid.
[154]*Homilies* (Coll. II) XLVIII.4.
[155]See infra.

maximalism of monastic life which rejects the world and human ways;[156] but he does not presume to impose it upon all Christians, nor even to make it into an intangible principle for monks.[157] The Fathers, he notes, "do not look upon those who cannot attain sufficient faith as terrible people . . . but at times they lovingly condescend to our weakness.[158] Thus St Barsanuphius, rather than spouting doctrine, gives to each the counsel that is appropriate to that person's spiritual condition, as does every spiritual father. He demands more of those who are nearer perfection and knows how to condescend to the weakness of others. To one of these, for example, he writes: "As for consulting a physician, only the perfect can turn everything over completely to God, even if it is painful; whereas the weak see a physician."[159] Origen held the same view: "Medicine is necessary in order to heal the body, if this is taken from the perspective of a simple, common life; and if one aspires to a higher life . . . one must be pious toward the almighty God and in the prayers addressed to Him."[160] The view of St Macarius, which many commentators have hastily listed among those of Tertullian, Tatian and Arnobius,[161] is in fact a much more nuanced position which turns out to be, upon careful reading, analogous to that of Origen, St Barsanuphius and St Gregory Palamas. Following the passage just cited he writes: "Most likely you will say: 'In order to heal the body, God has provided herbs from

---

[156]Loc. cit.
[157]Ibid.
[158]Ibid.
[159]*Letters* 770.
[160]*Adv. Celsus* VIII, 60.
[161]Cf. F. Kudlien, "Cynicism and Medicine," *Bulletin of the History of Medicine*, 43, 1974, 37-318. D.W. Amundsen, "Medicine and Faith in Early Christianity," 348. T.S. Miller, *The Birth of the Hospital in the Byzantine Empire*, 54, who also considers it to be dependent on the heretical doctrine of messalianism. The thesis of Macarius' messalianism, upheld by Villecourt, Dörries and Deppe, is rejected by many current specialists such as B. Krivocheine (*In the Light of Christ*, St Vladimir's Seminary Press, 1986, 31), P. Deseille (Introduction aux *Homélies spirituelles* de St Macaire, Bellefontaine, 1984, 12-17) and especially J. Meyendorff, who showed that the macarian writings are rather polemical writings against messalian deviations ("Messalianism or Anti-Messalianism? A Fresh Look at the Macarian Problem," *Kyriakon. Festschrift Johannes Quasten*, Münster Westf., 1970, vol. II, 585-590).

the earth and medicine, and he has provided the care of physicians for
the body's illnesses . . .' I agree that it is so; but be careful and understand in what manner and to whom this has been given, and for
whose sake God has made these things available by way of economy,
moved by his love for mankind and his supreme and infinite goodness . . . [God] has given these remedies to the people of this world
. . . for their comfort, the healing and care of the body, and he allowed
their use for all those who could not yet entrust themselves completely to God. But you, who lead a life of solitude, who have moved
toward Christ, who desire to be a son of God and to be born from on
high, of the Spirit . . . who have become a stranger in this world, you
must acquire a completely new faith, a new way of thinking and of
living, different from that of all other people of this world."[162]

Those who are perfect have no need of medicine because for them
God is all in all, and they incline themselves toward God in a direct
and unique way.[163] It is also because their spiritual state is such that
they are able to bear their illness or to obtain healing from God.[164]
Finally, it is because they are able, in this last instance, to remain
humble by avoiding the temptation of pride which is bound to arise
and lead them to consider their healing to be a result of their own
strength, to think of themselves as saints, to glory in their own miracles and to disdain any help that might come from others. Saint
Barsanuphius warns one of his correspondents: "If you do not resort
to physicians, beware of any thoughts of self-aggrandizement."[165]
Meanwhile St Diadochus of Photike recommends that spiritual
seekers call on physicians when they are ill "especially so that they do
not fall prey to vainglory and to the temptations of the devil that
cause some to boast that they have no need of physicians."[166] It is
often out of humility that the saints themselves resort to secular medicine though they could have obtained directly from God, through

---

[162]*Homilies* (Coll. II) XLVIII.5-6.
[163]Cf. St Gregory Palamas, loc. cit.
[164]Cf. St Barsanuphius, *Letters* 532.
[165]*Letters* 508.
[166]*One Hundred Chapters* 53.

prayer, the healing of their own illnesses or those of their disciples or visitors.[167]

It follows necessarily, therefore, that those who are not perfect must do the same. For a weak person to see a physician "is not a sin but humility, because he is weak enough to need to see a physician," notes St Barsanuphius.[168] Though his position is quite strict in principle, he appears far more flexible in practice, going so far as to entrust medical responsibilities to the future saint Dorotheus and encouraging him to pursue secular medicine.[169]

What actually seems important to saint Barsanuphius is that one never forget, every time one resorts to medicine, that it is always God who heals through them.[170]

A SPIRITUAL UNDERSTANDING OF SECULAR MEANS OF HEALING

From this perspective, the rigorist positions held by Tertullian, Tatian and Arnobius may themselves be interpreted in a positive sense which would qualify their influence. It seems they most feared that faith in physicians would take the place of faith in God, and that those who resorted to medicine would develop an idolatrous attitude of sorts, trusting in the material properties themselves. It is precisely to counter such a risk that Christians, as they adopt secular medicine, need to elaborate an understanding and a practice that does not contradict the fundamental truth that God is the only physician.

First and foremost, the Fathers emphasize that the remedies found in nature, or created from natural elements, as well as the art of discovering, extracting and making them, just like the art of applying them beneficially, all have their origin in God. They are all his gifts to mankind so that we, to the extent of our ability, might face the

---

[167]Cf., for example, John Moschus, *The Spiritual Meadow* 42, 65, 184. Palladius, *Lausiac History* XXIV.2; XXXV.11-12; XXXVIII.9. Theodoret of Cyrus, *History of the Monks of Syria* XIII.3. St John Chrysostom, *Letters to Olympiades* IV.1.

[168]*Letters* 770.

[169]Cf. *Letters* 327.

[170]Cf. *Letters* 129, 327, 508, 770.

conditions of physical existence in a fallen world, and to which our bodies have been subject since the fall.[171] "Each of the various arts was given to us by God to make up for what is lacking in nature . . . and this is certainly the case for medicine," wrote St Basil.[172] And he adds: "The body is subject to many illnesses whose causes are either internal or external . . . and it suffers at times from excess, at times from lack. This is why God, who governs our whole life, has given us medicine which removes what is in excess and supplies what is lacking."[173] "Having been bound to death through sin and, thereafter, to every illness, we obtained from God the relief which medicine procures for all who are ill. It is not by chance that the soil produces plants whose properties are especially suited to heal every illness; it is evident rather that the Creator wants them to be of use to us."[174] Theodoret of Cyrus even wrote that "while the pains that assail the body are many, the remedies against them are even more numerous for there are many ways which the art [of medicine] has discovered to fight each illness. If the Creator caused the earth to produce so many plants—not only edible ones but others that are not—it is precisely because man needs not only food but also remedies for his own healing. This is why we have among them some that we put to our own uses . . . while physicians gather others to make remedies that cure our ills, so that that which would be fatal if it were ingested becomes a remedy to take away our illness."[175] Because, as Origen points out, the Creator has not only placed in nature the remedies which man needed but, by endowing him with reason, has also given him the knowledge to put them to use."[176] The knowledge that a physician implements in arriving at a

---

[171]Cf. Origen, *Homilies on the Psalms 37*, 1, PG 12.1369. St Macarius, *Homilies* (Coll. II) XLVIII.5-6. St Basil, *Great Rules* 55.

[172]*Great Rules* 55. Cf. Theodoret of Cyrus, *Discourse on Providence* IV.

[173]Ibid.

[174]Ibid. St Diadochus of Photike even claims that God created them knowing we would have need of them: "As man's experience would one day lead him to develop the art of medicine, for this reason these remedies preexisted." (*One Hundred Chapters* 53).

[175]*Discourse on Providence* IV.

[176]*Homilies on Psalm 37*, 1, PG 12.1369. Cf. *Homilies on Numbers* XVIII.3. *Commentary on 3 Kings* XV.23.

diagnosis and prescribing a treatment, as well as that of a pharmacist who prepares the medication, is derived from the intelligence which God has bestowed upon man. As Origen inquires, "if all wisdom comes from the Lord [Sir 1:1], what science comes from him more than the science of health?"[177]

Thus, as St Basil notes, accepting medicine and its prescriptions allows one to "manifest the glory of God."[178] A physician, through his art as well as through the medicine he prescribes, is merely implementing the divine energies that were generously poured out by the Creator, in all created beings as well as in the human spirit. Medical science and its remedies shed their secular aspect as one recognizes that they are mediators of this divine providence that causes the light of God's glory to shine upon all things. Far from rivaling or paralleling religious means of healing, they are rather an indirect form of these, and it is ultimately revealed that there is but one physician: God. For it is only through his grace, his power, his virtues and his energies that physicians, whether believers or non-believers, whether knowingly or unknowingly, are able to act effectively, for good. Through these remedies God is the agent: he saves us "by means of visible things," as St Basil notes.[179] In the same way it is he who acts through the physician who operates "reasonably" (logikōs).[180] This is why St Barsanuphius writes: "It is in the Name of the Lord that we entrust ourselves to physicians, believing that he will effect our healing through them."[181]

HEALING COMES FROM GOD

It is clear that healing itself, while resulting from natural processes, actually comes from God. St Theophilus of Antioch brings this to the

---

[177]Cf. *Homilies on Numbers* XVIII.3.

[178]Loc. cit. Cf. Theodoret, loc. cit.

[179]Loc. cit.

[180]Cf. St Basil, loc. cit. For the Fathers, the deepest meaning of the term *logikōs* is "conforming to the Logos."

[181]*Letters* 508.

attention of Autolycus: "You may have fallen ill and lost weight, your strength and your appearance; but you found in God mercy and healing. You have regained your stature, your appearance and your strength: you do not know where your weight, appearance and strength had gone when they disappeared, neither do you know whence they were formed nor whence they came. But you will say: 'They came from the food and the liquids that have gone through the blood.' Very well! But this too is the work of God who has made it so, He and no other."[182]

Sirach already evoked these various notions: "Honor the physician with the honor due him, according to your need of him, for the Lord created him; for healing [the wisdom of the physician, according to the Hebrew text] comes from the Most High, and he will receive a gift from the king . . . The Lord created medicines from the earth, and a sensible man will not despise them . . . And he gave skill to men that he might be glorified in his marvelous works. By them he heals and takes away pain; the pharmacist makes of them a compound. His works will never be finished; and from him health is upon the face of the earth" (Sir 38:1-8).

The Christian attitude is thus diametrically opposed to naturalism and sees as an illusion the belief that the medical arts and remedies are, in and of themselves, good and effective means of healing. St Barsanuphius emphasizes that "without God, nothing avails, not even the physician."[183] And he adds: "Do not forget that without God there is no healing for anyone."[184]

This is why Christians, while they rely on physicians, see them simply as mediators.[185] They call on them in the name of God,[186] and it is through them, but from God, that they ask for healing. St Barsanuphius writes the following: "Those who resort to physicians, may they resort to them while relying on God, saying: 'It is in the

---

[182] *To Autolycus* I.13.
[183] *Letters* 770.
[184] *Letters* 327.
[185] Cf. St Basil, loc. cit.
[186] Cf. St Barsanuphius, *Letters* 508, 532.

name of God that we entrust ourselves to physicians, believing that
he will grant us healing through them'."[187] Likewise, when a Christian takes a prescription, he prays God that it might be effective. And
once he is healed, he prays God again in thanksgiving. On this subject St Basil notes the example of Hezeki'ah (2 Kg 20:7) who "did not
consider the cake or the fig to be the only cause of health and did not
attribute his healing thereto, but he gave thanks to God for having
also created figs."[188] When man fails to turn to God he is condemned
to a spiritual death, as was the case for King Asa (2 Chr 16:12-13): "In
the thirty-ninth year of his reign Asa was diseased in his feet, and his
disease became severe; yet even in his disease he did not seek the
Lord, but sought help from physicians. And he slept with his fathers,
dying in the forty-first year of his reign." This is also the pointed
reminder of Abba Macarius: "If a person is physically ill, if he does
not hope for help from above, as did Job and the paralytic, he has
blasphemed against the power of the Holy Trinity and has allowed a
place within himself for Satan."[189] Origen draws the following lesson
from the story of King Asa: "Those who have assumed piety resort to
doctors by seeing them as servants of God, knowing that He is the
one who gives medical science to mankind, just as He is the one who
made the plants grow in the earth and who put other [medicinal]
substances there. They know also that the art of the physician is in no
way efficacious without the will of God."[190]

As for Christian physicians, the most basic trait in their attitude
is the sense that they can do nothing of themselves nor merely by
means of their art. This is why they pray to God for inspiration before
making a diagnosis. And before they prescribe any course of treatment they ask God that it might be sufficient and efficacious, and
they invoke the power of God upon the sick, making themselves the
transparent media of His regenerative grace. "He who undertakes to
practice medicine must do so in the name of God and God will help

[187] *Letters* 508.
[188] Loc. cit.
[189] *Apophthegmata*, Am. 200.5.
[190] *Commentary on 3 Kg* XV.23.

him," says St Barsanuphius.[191] Concerning physicians, Sirach says: ". . . they too will pray to the Lord that he should grant them success in diagnosis and in healing, for the sake of preserving life" (Sir 38:14).

THE LIMITATIONS OF MEDICAL SCIENCE

These limitations curtail the potential presumption of physicians, of whom Sirach says: "[His] knowledge gives him high standing and wins him the admiration of the great" (Sir 38:8). To those who believe that the power to heal comes from themselves or from medical science alone, Job cries out: "As for you, you whitewash with lies; worthless physicians are you all" (Job 13:4).

Thus, while they recognize the value of science and of the medical profession, the Fathers clearly emphasize its limitations.[192] They often caution the sick against the temptation of regarding medicine and physicians as absolute, thus forgetting that God is ultimately the only physician and the sole source of all healing. St Isaac the Syrian therefore attributes the lowest order of knowledge to any science or technique "governed by the body," that is "preoccupied only with this world," and "does not see that the Providence of God directs us." Likewise he rates any knowledge that leads man to believe that "through his own effort and behavior, he has naturally within himself every good thing, the salvation that frees him from harm, the attentiveness that allows him to avoid the difficulty of so much adversity

---

[191]*Letters* 327.

[192]Among them, the inability of physicians to cure certain illnesses is strongly emphasized in many hagiographic texts, particularly those relating to unmercenary saints. Cf., among others, *Kosmas und Damianos*, ed. L. Deubner, Leipzig-Berlin, 1907, 16 (p. 138-29), 23 (p. 160-610). *Vita Sampsonis*, PG 115.284-288. See also Palladius, *Lausiac History* XXXVIII.9. *Life of St Theodore of Sykeon* 80b, 97, 121, 156. We must note that this powerlessness is pointed out by the evangelists Mark and Luke in their accounts of the woman with the flow of blood: ". . . a woman who had had a flow of blood for twelve years and could not be healed by any one . . ." (Lk 8:43); "And there was a woman who had a flow of blood for twelve years, and who had suffered much under many physicians, and had spent all that she had, and was no better but rather grew worse" (Mk 5:25-26).

that arises both secretly and openly." And so he says of those "who fancy that [knowledge] itself is the providence of all things, like those who say that there is no God ruling the visible world."[193]

St Barsanuphius writes: "We must not place our hope [in medicine], but in God who gives both life and death, who said: 'I wound and I heal' (Dt 32:39)."[194] St Basil likewise says that "when we resort to medicine we must beware not to attribute health and sickness to it exclusively,"[195] and again, "it is foolish to place one's hope for healing in physicians as we see it done by some unfortunate souls who do not hesitate to call them their saviors."[196] St Diadochus of Photike, while recommending the aid of physicians, says that "one must not however place one's hope for healing in them, but in our true Savior and Physician, Jesus Christ."[197]

By their very nature the medical arts have limitations, so that as "sciences" they bear only on phenomena and naturally lead to regarding illness as a reality in itself, independent of the person suffering from it. The latter is viewed as a "case," reduced to a set of symptoms and ultimately treated as an object. However, an ailing body is always that of a person; its condition is always connected to the soul, the psychological as well as the spiritual state of that person. Given the person's relationship to God and the spiritual meaning that illness may assume in such a setting, which encompasses not only the person's immediate condition but his destiny as well, it seems impossible to understand perfectly either the cause or the development of an illness merely by observing its symptoms.

The root cause of illness and the reasons for which it affects one person rather than another, at one particular time rather than another, most often lie beyond the ken of a clinician. This is because he is able to grasp only natural causes, whereas illness has a metaphysical cause as well, as St Basil reminds us: "The various infirmities

---

[193] *Ascetical Homilies* 63.
[194] *Letters* 508.
[195] Loc. cit.
[196] Ibid.
[197] *One Hundred Chapters* 53.

... do not all have causes against which the use of medicine may be deemed effective."[198]

The process of healing, from a clinical perspective, leaves the same issues unresolved: the variety of reactions to the same treatment, the disparity that often exists between the rate of healing and the cause or extent of the illness, the difficulty in healing benign illnesses and the "spontaneous" remission of severe ones. Mere science is often hard pressed to explain all of this and one must then refer to the sick person's own reality and destiny and to his relationship with God. Sometimes God saves a man directly and invisibly, apart from remedies, or together with them; at times it is in these remedies that his grace is active, sometimes quickly, sometimes slowly.[199] Whatever the circumstances, the healing is subject to the will of God: "God restores health to the sick whenever he wills," St Barsanuphius reminds us,[200] because his will tends toward what is spiritually most beneficial for each of us.

Man's entire nature and his eschatology, as these are depicted in Christian terms, reveal the limitations of medicine not only with regard to its ability to understand the illness or the sick person, but also with regard to its effective scope.

On the one hand, the relief brought by medicine can last only so long. Our corruptible bodies are bound to be affected by other illnesses, and ultimately by death. Theodoret of Cyrus notes that death "perturbs the physician and shows up the conceit of remedies."[201]

HAVE A CARE ALSO FOR THE HEALING OF THE SOUL

On the other hand, man is not merely a body. This is why, St Basil says, "Christians must avoid that which appears to direct their whole life toward caring for the body."[202] To be concerned strictly with the

---

[198]Loc. cit.
[199]Cf. St Basil, Loc. cit.
[200]*Letters* 770.
[201]*Discourse on Providence* VI. Cf. St Gregory Palamas, *Triads* II.1.10.
[202]Loc. cit.

body would amount to losing both body and soul for all eternity. By invoking God in times of illness, a Christian makes of these an occasion for the salvation of his body, but also, and more importantly, of his soul. St Basil also gives this advice: "In every instance, whether we follow the rules of medicine or, for reasons previously stated, we set them aside, we must always have in mind the will of God, work toward the good of the soul and fulfill the precepts of the Apostles: "So, whether you eat or drink, or whatever you do, do all to the glory of God" (1 Cor 10:31).[203] The important thing is to experience both the healing and the illness in God, whatever the means of healing may be.

Again, St Basil advises: "When the grace of healing is given to us . . . let us receive it gratefully, without distinguishing whether God has saved us in some invisible way, or whether he has done so by way of visible things."[204] In health as in sickness, man must not lose sight of the ultimate goal, the complete and definitive salvation of his entire being in Christ. To the young Panteleimon, who wanted to become a physician, St Hermolaus—his spiritual father, who was also a physician—said that "Esclapius, Hippocrates and Galen truly conveyed secrets to heal the body's ills and, for a time, to preserve the health and the life that must necessarily be lost, but that Jesus Christ was a far more excellent physician in that he healed the illness of both body and soul, and he gave eternal life."[205] It is from this perspective that all Christian physicians have been sanctified by acting, within their practice, in accordance with the will of God,[206] committing

---

[203]Ibid.

[204]Ibid.

[205]"Les petits bollandistes," *Lives of the Saints* (Paris, 1873), t. IX, 54.

[206]In addition to the holy unmercenary physicians, whom the Church mentions in the prothesis of the liturgy and of whom she begs the intercession in the service of holy unction (Cosmos and Damian, Cyrus and John, Panteleimon and Hermolaus, Samson and Diomedes, Photius and Anicetus, Thalelus and Tryphon), we must note the existence within the Orthodox Church of a category of physicians, known to this day in Greece as *iatrophilosophoi* (literally, philosopher physicians), who are recognized primarily for their theological learning and their piety (see S. Harakas, "'Rational Medicine,'" *op. cit.*, p. 163. D.J. Constantelos, "Physician-priests in the Medieval Greek Church," p. 149). On of the most famous was Eustratios Argenti

themselves above all to proclaiming to those in their care the complete healing of human nature in Christ. Following his example they reveal, through the miraculous healing of the body, the miraculous healing of the soul. While they continue to display the attributes of the medical arts, they break through its limitations by revealing to all the original, transcendent source of all healing. They make of their practice and of its assets a means for conveying the grace that is manifested in the miracles they perform as these become signs, tokens of a deeper and fuller healing brought about by Christ.[207]

Every medical intervention becomes both a symbol and a calling. In turning to the sick, the physicians invite them to consider God's mercy and to turn to Him. As they heal their bodies, they invite the sick to find healing for their souls.[208] As they change illness to health, they encourage a conversion of their hearts.[209] Thus, they reveal within the medical arts a symbolic meaning that transcends its primary function without ever denying it. As St Basil writes: "The medical arts symbolize the art of healing souls"[210] and must be understood first and foremost as "a figure of the care that we owe our souls."[211] The Fathers have made abundant use of this symbol, referring to the study and practice of spirituality as a medicine for the soul.[212]

(1687-1757) (see T. Ware, *Eustratios Argenti, a Study of the Greek Church under Turkish Rule*, Oxford, 1964, 45-47).

[207]It is noteworthy that, in their icons, the holy physicians are depicted with the instruments specific to their profession. These are represented according to the usual inverse perspective, but they are also washed in the uncreated Light (of divine energies) that radiates from their faces. This is not done strictly for typological or canonical reasons; the icons thereby express the fact that these saints have achieved a spiritual integration of their art, and also that they have made of their practice a means of revealing higher realities by allowing divine grace to operate.

[208]In his letter "to Eustathios, the great physician," St Basil congratulates him for acting in this way: "You remove for yourself the bounds of love for mankind, for you do not limit the benefits of your art to the body, but you consider also the healing of illnesses of the soul" (*Letters* CLXXXIX.1).

[209]Thus, in hagiographic accounts, the healing of the sick is always associated with their conversion, as R. Aigrain emphasizes in *L'Hagiographie* (Paris, 1953), 185-192.

[210]Loc. cit.

[211]Ibid.

[212]This aspect was studied in our *Thérapeutique des maladies spirituelles*.

THE HEALING OF THE BODY SYMBOLIZES AND FORETELLS THE HEALING OF OUR WHOLE BEING

The Fathers place within this greater spiritual context not only the healings that come about through medicine, but also those effected through religious means. In either case, the healing of physical illnesses always raises the issue of spiritual illnesses. Every time the Fathers ask God to heal the body of a sick person, they ask Him also to heal the soul and to grant him salvation. This perspective is founded on the teaching and practice of Christ himself.

Through the physical healings he performs, Christ manifests his mercy and compassion toward those who are suffering, together with his desire to relieve them of their illness and physical infirmity. But beyond the healing of the body, he aims to heal the soul—thereby demonstrating its greater importance—and shows those who come to him only for physical healing how much more he has to offer than other physicians and healers.[213] As St John Chrysostom says: "Jesus Christ desires most of all to heal our spiritual illnesses, since he heals our bodies only to go on thereafter to healing our souls."[214] Thus the paralytic—and those carrying him—(Mt 9:1-8; Mk 2:1-12; Lk 5:17-26) comes to Christ only to be healed of his physical infirmities, "wishing only for bodily health."[215] But instead of granting his request, Jesus says: "Take heart, my son; your sins are forgiven." It is only after the objections of a few scribes ("Why does this man speak thus? It is blasphemy!") that Jesus also frees the man from his physical infirmity. We see here that the healing of the body takes second place. It is specifically the visible sign (the only thing accessible to unbelievers, represented here by the scribes) of the greater healing that Christ effects within the soul.[216] Essentially, it symbolizes the external manifestation of the spiritual regeneration of the inner man, and is the clear revelation of Christ's power to accomplish this process. It is so

---

[213]Cf. Origen, *Adv. Celsus* I.68.
[214]*Homilies on Matthew* XXIX.2.
[215]Ibid.
[216]St John Chrysostom, *Homilies on Matthew* XXIX.1-2.

"that you may know that the Son of Man has authority on earth to forgive sins" that he says to the paralytic: "Rise!" (Mt 9:6; Mk 2:10; Lk 5:24), and then heals his physical infirmity.

ILLNESSES OF THE SOUL ARE MORE SERIOUS THAN THOSE OF THE BODY

In the eyes of the One who sounds the very depths of our hearts with a view to the salvation of our entire being for all eternity, spiritual illness is indeed far more serious than physical illness.[217] This is so even while the former remains, by its very nature, imperceptible to those who lack discernment, and while its detrimental effects are not as immediately detectable. After having healed the paralytic at the pool of Beth'zatha (Jn 5:1-9), Christ said to him: "Sin no more, that nothing worse befall you." (Jn 5:14). This "something worse" would be sin itself and its consequences, since the illness of the body, while it may lead to physical death, is not in itself an obstacle to salvation. It can affect only one's "outer nature" (2 Cor 4:16). Illness of the soul, however, hinders man's entire being, body and soul, from being saved. It is an obstacle to the renewal of the "inner nature," to the emergence of the "new man" born of the Spirit who manifests in his soul and in his body (2 Cor 4:10, 11) the life of Jesus that comes from the Father and makes of him a "new creation" (2 Cor 5:17) destined for all eternity to rejoice in the blessings of the Kingdom. It keeps mankind within the flesh that is "against the Spirit" (Gal 5:17) and from which one can reap only corruption (Gal 6:8) and death (Rom 8:13). This is why Christ says: ". . . do not fear those who kill the body but cannot kill the soul [meaning, among other things, physical illness]; rather fear him who can destroy both soul and body in hell" (Mt 10:28) (meaning the just Judge who allows those who have chosen not to ask him for healing to suffer the consequences of their spiritual illness).

---

[217]Cf. St Gregory of Nazianzus, *Oration* XIV.18.

THE RELATIVE NATURE OF PHYSICAL HEALTH

While bodily illness itself cannot affect man in his essential reality as
a new creation nor in his eternal destiny, bodily health is only of relative value with regard to that reality and destiny. On the one hand,
if a person remains ill in his soul, the health of the body is of no avail
since he remains "in the flesh" (cf. Jn 6:63) and does not use his members to the glory of God. It does not keep him ultimately from per-
ishing "in Gehenna." On the other hand, the health of the body in
this world can only be precarious and ephemeral. "All flesh is like
grass and all its glory like the flower of grass. The grass withers, and
the flower falls" (1 Pet 1:24; Isa 40:6). As long as man lives in this
world, his current condition as "man of dust" (1 Cor 15:47-49) and
"physical body" (1 Cor 15:44, 46) remains subject to corruption and
must suffer death because of sin (cf. Rom 5:12). ". . . our outer nature
is wasting away" (2 Cor 4:16); ". . . the earthly tent we live in" must be
"destroyed" (2 Cor 5:1).

THE PROMISE OF FUTURE INCORRUPTIBILITY AND IMMORTALITY

As Christ heals those who are physically ill and restores them to
health, his purpose for them is something far greater: to free them
once and for all from corruption and death by raising their bodies
which, by the power of God, have become incorruptible and immortal, and to bestow upon them, in this new body as in their souls, true
life for all eternity. "So we do not lose heart. Though our outer nature
is wasting away, our inner nature is being renewed every day. For this
slight momentary affliction is preparing for us an eternal weight of
glory beyond all comparison, because we look not to the things that
are seen but to the things that are unseen; for the things that are seen
are transient, but the things that are unseen are eternal. For we know
that if the earthly tent we live in is destroyed, we have a building from
God, a house not made with hands, eternal in the heavens" (2 Cor
4:16-5:1). Henceforth, the miracles that Christ performs seem to be
primarily visible signs of this coming restoration, where our bodies

will be healed once and for all of every illness and we will experience a perfect and permanent health. By raising some in their very bodies and by healing others in their members, Christ, writes St Irenaeus, "prefigured the eternal through the temporal and revealed himself to be the One with the power to give to the work which he fashioned both healing and life, that we might also believe the word concerning the resurrection."[218]

CHRIST CAME ALSO TO SAVE THE BODY

Unlike the pagan pseudo-deities that remain indifferent to the fate of mortals, or the "sages" who consider only the release of the soul and scorn the body which they see as a tomb into which the soul has fallen from its original state and from which it must seek to "free" itself as quickly as possible, Christ manifests the love of God for man and comes to save him in his entirety, body and soul. He does so not only in this life where he calls man to know, in both body and soul, the first-fruits of divine blessings, but also in the hereafter where, once his body has been raised and made incorruptible, he can rejoice in them fully in his entire being for all eternity.[219] The Son of the Father, the Word of God, He who is "in the form of God, did not count equality with God a thing to be grasped" (Phil 2:6) and deigned to

---

[218]*Adv. Haer.* V.13.1. Cf. Tertullian, *On the Resurrection* 38. In this context it is common in several scriptural passages that recount the miraculous healings performed by Christ or the Apostles, to find use of the verb *sōzein* (cf. Mt 9:22; 14:36; Mk 5:34; 6:56; 10:52; Lk 8:48, 50; 17:19; 18:42; Acts 4:9; 14:9). The term, as we have already pointed out, has the double meaning "to heal" and "to save." And again the verb *egeirein* (cf. Mt 8:15; 9:6; Mk 1:31; 2:11; 9:27; Lk 5:24; 6:8; Jn 5:8; Acts 3:6-7), which also has two meanings: rising up from an illness and rising from the dead; in other words to be resurrected. For both these expressions, the second meaning is discernable behind the first when the first is indicated by the context. Conversely, the dual meaning reveals salvation and resurrection as the healing of human nature.

[219]Cf. *Hagioritic Tome*, PG 150.1233B-D. St Symeon the New Theologian, *Catechesis*, XV.73.74. St Maximus, *Ambigua*, PG 91.1088C: "remaining fully man by virtue of his nature, in both soul and body, [man] becomes fully god, in both body and soul, through divine grace and splendor and the beatifying glory he so properly assumes."

become flesh (Jn 1:14). By enhypostatizing our entire human nature
in its fallen state (save for sin), by becoming a "mere man" (Heb 4:15)
and thus assuming a passible human soul as well as a corruptible
human body, subject to illness, suffering and death, "He assumed all
things that all things might be healed."[220] By suffering in his human
body the consequences of the sin of Adam, yet without sinning himself, he assumed the corruptibility of our nature, even to accepting to
suffer the Passion on the Cross and to die "in his body of flesh" (Col
1:21) with his soul dwelling in hell and his body in the tomb. Yet while
remaining God without change, he did not allow the powers of hell
to have dominion over his soul, nor his body to be subject to corruption (Acts 2:31), but he despoiled hell and destroyed corruption. And
so within himself he freed our nature from the tyranny of the devil
whom he annihilated (Heb 2:14), and from the grasp of sin which he
destroyed (Rom 6:6), freeing us from slavery to corruption. By his
death he has conquered death, by his Resurrection he has given life
to our entire nature, body and soul, and by his Ascension into heaven
he has glorified our entire being and seated it at the right hand of the
Father. And it is with this same renewed nature that he will return in
glory in the end times to judge the world.

Through Christ's victory, death is no longer an end for man.
Specifically it is no longer a definitive separation of the body from the
soul nor an irreparable dissolution. Henceforth, as St John Chrysostom says, death is only the death of corruption and the destruction of
death.[221] If man must still die, it is not that his life comes to an end,
but that death for him is transcended, that he might live again and be
raised up to put on incorruptibility and immortality.[222] Because that
which is sown "does not come to life unless it dies" (1 Cor 15:36) "nor
does the perishable inherit the imperishable (1 Cor 15:50).

---

[220]St John of Damascus, *The Orthodox Faith* III.20. Again, he says: "He has
taken me completely and has fully united himself to me, to give me complete salvation, for he cannot heal what he has not assumed" (ibid., 6). St Gregory of Nazianzus
says likewise: "What is not assumed is not healed, and that which is united to God
is saved" (*Letters* CI).

[221]*Homilies on the Resurrection of the dead* 7. Cf. *Commentary on Psalm XLVIII.*5.

[222]*That Death is a Blessing* 15.

Through Christ, with Christ (1 Thess 4:14) and in Christ (1 Cor
15:22), through the power of the Spirit (Rom 8:11), God will bestow
life upon the dead and raise their bodies. He will heal them from
every ill, according to the word He spoke to the Prophet Isaiah: "Thy
dead shall live, their bodies shall rise. O dwellers in the dust, awake
and sing for joy!" (Is 26:19). The body will be delivered from its former infirmities and will recover its original integrity. On this subject,
Tertullian writes: "If the flesh is to be snatched from destruction, how
much more will it be healed of its infirmities . . . If we are transformed
unto glory, how much more will we be unto this singular integrity!
Thus the resurrection of the dead is nothing other than the restoration of their entire being, that they might not remain dead in that
part which is not raised."[223]

After raising the body and restoring its integrity, God will make
it incorruptible and immortal, "for this perishable nature must put on
the imperishable, and this mortal nature must put on immortality"
(1 Cor 15:53). It is then that "we shall be changed" (1 Cor 15:52). But
this does not mean that we will put on a body other than the one we
had on earth: we are dealing neither with metempsychosis nor with
reincarnation. The Fathers place a great emphasis on this point.[224]
Each person will be clothed with his own body, but it will be free of
the imperfections, the weakness, the corruptibility and the mortality
that are characteristic of its current nature. "So is it with the resurrection of the dead. What is sown is perishable, what is raised is
imperishable. It is sown in dishonor, it is raised in glory. It is sown in
weakness, it is raised in power" (1 Cor 15:42-43). It will no longer exist
in its current material mode and thus will no longer be subject to
those exigencies, those necessities and limitations of every kind,[225]

---

[223] *On the Resurrection* 57.

[224] Cf., for example, St John Chrysostom, *Homilies on 1 Corinthians* XLI.1 and
XLII.2; *Homilies on 2 Corinthians* X.2-3. St Irenaeus, *Adv. Haer.* V.2.3. Tertullian, *On
the Resurrection* 52; 53; 55; 60; 62. St Gregory of Nyssa, *The Creation of Man* XXVII,
XXVIII.

[225] Cf. St Gregory of Nyssa, *De mortuis*, PG 46.532, 536. St Gregory Palamas,
Triads I.3.36.

having become much like Christ's body.[226] Without ceasing to be a body, it will "receive a form like that of the soul"[227] and, from the "physical body" it once was, it will become a "spiritual body."[228] It will be perfectly united to the soul[229] and entirely transparent to the spiritual energies.[230] According to Christ's own words, after the resurrection we will be "like angels in heaven" (Mk 12:25 // Mt 22:30 // Lk 20:35-36).[231]

In this new state, the body will no longer bear the image of the earthly but that of the heavenly (1 Cor 15:49) and thus will no longer be subject to any form of corruption: it will no longer experience illness,[232] nor physical suffering,[233] nor deterioration of any kind.[234]

Then man will experience in his body a perfect, complete and permanent health, that he might receive—in this body as in his soul—the fullness of grace. Thus he will become, through his entire being, a participant in divine nature (2 Pet 1:4), to rejoice eternally in divine blessings with all his members and with every means that God has bestowed upon him from the beginning when He created him to "become god." He will then find Himself led to perfection by the power of the Spirit that will transfigure and enliven him.

---

[226]Cf. 231 S. John Chrysostom, *Homilies on Philippians* XIII.2. After his resurrection, Christ thus demonstrates that the human body in its new state transcends material laws, by entering despite "the doors being shut" (Jn 20:19, 26), or by vanishing suddenly (Lk 24:31). If he eats in the company of the disciples (Lk 24:41-43) it is not out of necessity but by economy, that they might not believe it was a ghost that appeared before them (cf. Mk 6:49; Lk 24:37). A hymn from the tone eight Sunday matins says: Your disciples "believed they saw a spirit. But you relieved their troubled souls by showing them your hands and feet; and as they still disbelieved, you sat down to eat with them."

[227]St Maximus, *Mystagogy* VII.

[228]Cf. St Gregory Palamas, loc. cit.

[229]Cf. St Maximus, *On the Divine Names* I.4, PG 4.197.

[230]Cf. St Gregory Palamas, loc. cit.

[231]Ibid.

[232]Cf. John Chrysostom, *Homilies on the consolation of death* I.6. St Ammonas, *Letters* I.2.

[233]Cf. St john Chrysostom, *Homilies on 2 Corinthians* X.1 and 2; *Homilies on 1 Corinthians* XLI.1. St Ammonas, *Letters* I.2.

[234]Cf. St Gregory of Nyssa, loc. cit. Tertullian, *op. cit.*, 57.

In this way, the body will fulfill its ultimate destiny of being dei-fied along with the soul in the human hypostasis. Man, writes St Maximus, "while remaining fully man by nature in body and soul, becomes fully god in his soul and his body, through the divine grace and splendor of beatifying glory."[235]

---

[235]St Maximus the Confessor, *Ambigua*, PG 91.1088C.